T0277290

"*Becoming Happy & Healthy* is a helpful guide to anyone left reeling from their choices or who is confused and fearful of what's up ahead. Jeanine is a bright light in her generation who brings insight and truth in this stunning debut. It's the book I wish I had when I was starting out. Gift this book to all the young women in your life. They will be so blessed!"

Lysa TerKeurst, #1 New York Times bestselling author,
president of Proverbs 31 Ministries

"I have watched Jeanine mature as a Jesus follower and lead others to a happier and healthier lifestyle. In this book she is not only honest about her struggles but is also a trusted guide for us through our struggles. In the pages ahead she will show you where true happiness is found and will help you enjoy the journey there."

Jonathan Pokluda, pastor of Harris Creek Baptist Church,
bestselling author, host of the Becoming Something podcast

"If you've ever felt like happiness and true fulfillment were out of reach, Jeanine Amapola will change your perspective. In her practical and inspiring new book, *Becoming Happy & Healthy*, Jeanine writes openly about her own emptiness and Christ-centered journey toward a life full of meaning. If you're tired of accepting less than God's best for your life, stop settling and start reading."

Craig Groeschel, pastor of Life.Church, New York Times
bestselling author

"Jeanine builds a beautiful vision of how to live a life pleasing to God. This is not just words for her—this is her life. She follows Jesus and loves him deeply."

Jennie Allen, New York Times bestselling author
of Find Your People and Get Out of Your Head,
founder and visionary of IF:Gathering

"I've had the honor of knowing Jeanine for the past decade both personally and professionally. Following her through many seasons of life, I can truly say she is one of the few people I look up to. Although Jeanine is just a phone call away for me, I am excited for others to know her on a deeper level through this book. Jeanine has made an impact on my life, and I pray the world can now experience a greater impact through her wisdom!"

Dani Austin, founder of Divi Official

Becoming
Happy &
Healthy

Becoming
Happy &
Healthy

Real Life Advice on Friendship, Dating, Career, and Everything Else You Care About

Jeanine Amapola

BETHANYHOUSE

a division of Baker Publishing Group
Minneapolis, Minnesota

© 2024 by Jeanine Amapola

Published by Bethany House Publishers
Minneapolis, Minnesota
BethanyHouse.com

Bethany House Publishers is a division of
Baker Publishing Group, Grand Rapids, Michigan

Printed in the United States of America

Library of Congress Cataloging-in-Publication Data
Names: Amapola, Jeanine, author.
Title: Becoming happy & healthy : real life advice on friendship, dating, career, and everything else you care about / Jeanine Amapola.
Other titles: Becoming happy and healthy
Description: Minneapolis, Minnesota : Bethany House Publishers, a division of Baker Publishing Group, [2024] | Includes bibliographical references.
Identifiers: LCCN 2023037704 | ISBN 9780764241772 (cloth) | ISBN 9781493445103 (ebook)
Subjects: LCSH: Christian women—Religious life. | Happiness—Religious aspects—Christianity. | Health—Religious aspects—Christianity. | Friendship—Religious aspects—Christianity. | Decision making—Religious aspects—Christianity.
Classification: LCC BV4527 .A476 2024 | DDC 248.8/43—dc23/eng/20231024
LC record available at https://lccn.loc.gov/2023037704

Unless otherwise indicated, Scripture quotations are from THE HOLY BIBLE, NEW INTERNA-TIONAL VERSION®, NIV® Copyright © 1973, 1978, 1984, 2011 by Biblica, Inc.® Used by permission. All rights reserved worldwide.

Scripture quotations labeled ESV are from The Holy Bible, English Standard Version® (ESV®), copyright © 2001 by Crossway, a publishing ministry of Good News Publishers. Used by permission. All rights reserved. ESV Text Edition: 2016

Scripture quotations labeled KJV are from the King James Version of the Bible.

Scripture quotations labeled NABRE are from the New American Bible, revised edition © 2010, 1991, 1986, 1970 Confraternity of Christian Doctrine, Washington, DC, and are used by permission of the copyright owner. All rights reserved. No part of the New American Bible may be reproduced in any form without permission in writing from the copyright owner.

Scripture quotations labeled NASB are from the New American Standard Bible® (NASB), copyright © 1960, 1962, 1963, 1968, 1971, 1972, 1973, 1975, 1977, 1995 by The Lockman Foundation. Used by permission. www.Lockman.org

Scripture quotations labeled NKJV are from the New King James Version®. Copyright © 1982 by Thomas Nelson. Used by permission. All rights reserved.

Scripture quotations labeled NLT are taken from the Holy Bible, New Living Translation, copyright © 1996, 2004, 2015 by Tyndale House Foundation. Used by permission of Tyndale House Publishers, Inc., Carol Stream, Illinois 60188. All rights reserved.

The events described reflect the recollection of the author and may differ from others' recollections. Names and minor details have been omitted in some instances to protect the identities of the people involved.

Cover design by Micah Kandros Design

Published in association with The Bindery Agency, www.TheBinderyAgency.com.

Baker Publishing Group publications use paper produced from sustainable forestry practices and post-consumer waste whenever possible.

24 25 26 27 28 29 30   7 6 5 4 3 2 1

To my family; my husband, Kaleb; and all my friends
who have supported me throughout this journey, thank you.
I couldn't have done this without your prayers,
support, and belief in me.

Contents

Contents

Foreword

Has happiness ever felt unattainable and impossible?

It has for me.

I remember when I graduated from college and all my friends started getting married, having babies, and working their dream jobs. Meanwhile, I was going through a breakup, struggling with contentment and purpose in my job, ordering Chick-fil-A every night, and lying in bed crying myself to sleep.

Maybe you can relate. Maybe you feel far from being your *happiest and healthiest* self. It's easy to feel left behind, overlooked, and left out when there are comparison opportunities all around us, especially with social media at our fingertips. Maybe those around you feel happy and healthy (or at least they give off that vibe), but meanwhile you feel stuck, bound, confused, sad, lonely, and frustrated. Well, you're not alone. I have felt that way more times than I would like to admit, and my guess is that you have this book in your hands because you too have asked and wondered questions like:

When is it my turn to be happy?

How do I break free from shame and secret sin?

How do I find and maintain healthy friendships and relationships?

11

How can I be confident?
How do I grow in my faith?

If you are asking questions like these, good news: my best friend Jeanine wrote this book for you.

Jeanine and I first got to know each other after getting set up on a "friend date." We had mutual friends, and they knew we would hit it off and become besties. So, we decided to meet up. We ended up going to dinner and talking for, I kid you not, five hours. I left our dinner and called my mom and said, "I just met my new best friend."

There is something special about Jeanine. She loves Jesus and wants her life and moments on earth to matter and make a difference, but she is also *fun* (and happy!). We shared our secrets and struggles, and our conversations got deep quick. We laughed until we cried. And that was just the beginning of our friendship journey. We ended up becoming roommates (after I convinced her to move to Texas and live with me!), and it was two of the best years of my life. During that time, we traveled all over and made fun memories we will never forget, but most importantly we sharpened each other in becoming holier, happier, and healthier.

We walked through intense highs and lows: breakups, job transitions, friend and family hardships, adventures and travel, and meeting our now husbands. We challenged each other and called each other higher. And day after day, I saw Jeanine live out the message she preaches: becoming happy and healthy. I watched as she would start every morning the same with her banana pancakes and Jesus time, immediately followed by her going to the gym for some hard-core workout. After that, it seemed like she had more hours in the day than everyone else: she would somehow find time to record a podcast, go on a walk and encourage a friend, record social media videos, stop by and see her family, fix something with our house (it kept having problems), write a chapter of her book, and find time to catch up and be intentional with me. I even asked her a few times how she did it all, and she would always humbly reply, "I'm still figuring it out too!" I wondered if she had some secret superpower. But the more I got to know Jeanine, the more I saw she had two very important principles down:

She knew what mattered most.
She built healthy habits.

Jeanine and I always liked to joke that she was the grace to my truth. Not only did she show me how awesome creating healthy habits could be in life, but she also helped me embrace emotion and lead with vulnerability. She showed me that true strength is not perfectionism and secrecy but rather living in the light and in community, leaning on God's Word for all the answers to the problems that most of the time I created. When I started dating my husband, Grant, as soon as I got back from our first date, I ran into her room and cried, exclaiming, "I just met my husband!" Throughout the relationship, she would hold me accountable with our purity, and when we were going through a hard time, she would pray with me. And months later, when she went on her first date with Kaleb, she ran into my room, jumped on my bed, and with a big smile on her face, exclaimed, "I'm going to marry that man!"

I have seen her grow into a woman who knows who she is in Christ, living out this message—*becoming happy and healthy*—from the way she pursues Jesus to the way she loves her friends to the way she disciplines her mind, body, and soul. Jeanine is an amazing writer, podcast host, and social media influencer, but she's even more amazing at being a friend. And when you read this book, you will see what I mean. You will feel like you are talking with a friend. A friend who leads with her own vulnerability, insecurities, and struggles, and a friend who cares for you and wants you to be the best you can be. This book is real, authentic, honest, practical, and could change the way you see the world, yourself, and God.

Jeanine tackles some of the big topics we all struggle with or face: contentment in our current season, how to overcome loneliness and lies, and how to approach dating, careers, and friendships God's way. In each chapter you will find practical tips and self-evaluating questions that meet you where you are and challenge you to take steps toward becoming happier and healthier. This book speaks to the inspired heart and the weary heart. It will challenge you whether you are strong in your faith or doubting and questioning what you believe. My prayer is that as you read *Becoming Happy & Healthy* you will believe that just like Ephesians 3:20 says, there is abundantly more for you and that you—yes *you*—can live happy and healthy too.

Madison Prewett Troutt

Introduction

There I was in Los Angeles, California, at twenty-five years old. My idea of where I would be when I was twenty-five looked like this: marrying my dream guy, having a family, financially crushing it, being successful on social media, and maybe even living in a gorgeous big, white house by the beach with a fluffy goldendoodle running around. I'd thought surely by now I'd be happy, healthy, and thriving in my so-called *best life*. But instead, there I was: heartbroken and crying alone on my one-bedroom apartment living room floor. The carpet needed vacuuming badly. The dishes were piling up in the sink. I had hardly eaten in days; all I did was sulk and cry. I had just come out of a really painful and confusing relationship that I thought was leading toward marriage. I was unsure about my future. Insecure about myself. Unexpectedly lonely. Feeling a sense of disappointment in God and myself. Coping in unhealthy ways. And straying farther from God than I wanted to be.

Sitting there, I glanced at my unopened Bible, my angry journal entries, and the messiness in my apartment. *How did I get here?* This is not what I signed up for. I thought everything would work out for me if I just manifested it enough. Boy, I was wrong. I wanted to seek God more but just couldn't get there in my own strength. I knew something had to change.

Eventually, a month later, I managed to get myself out of my apartment and take a road trip. I headed to San Diego for the weekend, and that's when I got "the call." The call that forever changed my life.

It was August 2019, and I was at lunch with some friends when my phone rang. To my surprise, it was two of my guy friends, Daniel and Brett. I was shocked to see their names pop up on my phone since I had not spoken to them in a while, but I was eager to find out why they were calling me. I jumped out of my seat, excused myself from my friends, and answered curiously, "Hello?"

Brett and Daniel responded, "Jeanine! We are so glad you picked up! We're calling you because we have a proposal for you . . . just hear us out."

"Okay . . . you're making me nervous, but let's hear it!"

Brett and Daniel swiftly answered back, "Okay, get this . . . three-hundred-dollar round-trip tickets to Spain. While there, we'd go to Israel for a week, then go back to Spain on December fourth through the fifteenth. But here's the catch: it's a flight deal that you have to book by *tonight*. What do you think?"

I was so caught off guard! I needed a second to process it, but I was honored that they thought to invite me. I had never done something like this before. Israel and Spain? Two countries I had only dreamt of going to, and now I had the chance to go with some of my amazing friends?

I responded, "Oh my gosh! I mean, wow, this sounds so fun! Once I check the flights and my calendar, I'll let you know!"

I rushed to my friends' house that night to use their Wi-Fi, searched for all the details, made some calls, and booked the flight that night! My San Diego friends thought I'd lost my mind. I mean, maybe I did! *What did I just sign up for?* I thought to myself. I thought this trip was just going to be a fun little vacay with a group of friends, but it ended up being more than I ever expected.

December rolled around, and I got on my flight, enthusiastic to meet my current friends and some new ones too. I landed in Spain smelly, jet-lagged, hungry, and sore from sitting for ten-plus hours, but I had so much excitement for finally arriving in this new country that it all didn't matter. I joyfully ran up to the group at the airport, hugged Daniel and Brett, and met the rest of the group. The group had six guys and two girls, including myself. The week began to unfold by going on a five-mile run around town, laughing and dancing to Spanish music at a lively restaurant, and befriending the locals.

But the week was more than just fun. At dinners, our group would read the Bible together, pray for one another, and ask each other challenging questions. We would pray for random people on the streets, listen to each other's untold stories, and cry to one another about current things in our lives. I had never experienced this before.

Men who pray and cry?

A group of people who genuinely care for me?

People who don't want to get drunk but would rather just go dance and have a good time?

This was all new for me. I began to feel things I had never felt before.

We stayed in Spain for two nights, then headed off to Israel to join another group of Christians to learn more about Jesus. To see where he walked, where he taught, where he was persecuted and then rose again.

It was an eye-opening week for me. I cried many, many times. I felt the presence of God again. I could hear his voice again. And I began to rethink my whole life. I knew I was empty. I knew I couldn't do this on my own anymore. I knew I was trying to be this "perfect" Christian all in my own strength. I knew I needed Jesus, and badly.

Jesus began to reveal himself to me in the most surreal way that week—so much so that, by the end of the week, we all had an opportunity to get baptized, and I took it. I grew up Christian and had been baptized as a kid, but I decided as an adult, I'm going all in. I am no longer going my way, but *his* way. I got baptized in the Jordan River, the very same river that Jesus himself was baptized in. This day marked my life forever. I cried and felt so free! I went under the water and said good-bye to my old self, and I came out a new person (2 Corinthians 5:17).

I surrendered my life to Jesus and never imagined I would be here today writing about it all. I could cry thinking about it, because since that day, my life has been nothing but better. If I told my college self where I am at now and where God has taken me, she would never believe me, because my journey has not been glamorous or easy. But I've taken many steps to heal and become happy and healthy.

Maybe you are currently where I was in 2019: lost, confused, addicted, distant from God, sad, heartbroken, lonely, disliking yourself, unsure of what to do next, and simply seeking some guidance on some of life's biggest decisions and struggles. That's where this book comes in. I want to help you become happy and healthy in all aspects of life—God's way, because I have found that his way is the best way. Unfortunately, it took me a lot of wrong turns to see that, but my hope and prayer is that I can help you avoid those same mistakes and learn from them.

Just like my friends reached out to me to take me on an adventure of a lifetime, I am reaching out to you. But we aren't going to Spain. This trip is actually a journey through your heart and soul, right where you are in this moment, with all the struggles that you may face as you make decisions about your future, your relationships, your career, your habits, and your self-image.

That's why I wrote this book. This is the book that I wish I'd had back when I was in the deepest valleys of my life. Toni Morrison once shared, "If you find a book you really want to read but it hasn't been written yet, then you must write it."[1]

So that's what I did. I wrote the book I needed.

Because I think you may need it too.

This is a guide that I hope you come back to over and over to help you make better choices, date well, make friendships, live life to the fullest, navigate insecurities, overcome shame, take care of your body, be bold in your faith, and so much more! Think of me as your big sister and friend throughout this journey, guiding you along the way.

Throughout this book, I will show you how I overcame my own struggles, lack of identity, broken relationships, insecurities, negative thoughts, secrets, and dark moments to eventually become more free, joyful, and healthy. I will share the deepest parts of my heart, my thoughts, and my life in this book. The good, the bad, and the ugly. Stories I've never shared with the world before, all with the purpose of helping you, because I believe in you. No matter what your story is or how bad you think it is, there is hope.

I challenge you to read this with friends, ask each other what you think, and discuss each chapter together. Why not grow together? It's more fun that way! If you decide not to, that's okay too! The "Make It Real in Your Life" section at the end of each chapter has questions to ask yourself and to journal about. Be honest with yourself and see your growth along the way!

Before we dive in, I want to note something crucial—being happy and healthy is not a finish line but a journey. We are always a work in progress. Part of this journey of becoming happier and healthier is knowing that it will be difficult at times. There will be highs and lows. It won't always look linear, but we are on the path of progress, not perfection. God never said we wouldn't face trials and tribulations, but instead promised that he would never leave us along the way (Hebrews 13:5). We're on this journey of becoming happier and healthier together!

Shall we begin? Pack your bags!

1

Faith

How to Find and Follow God

Welcome to the journey, friend. I'm excited you're here. We are going to cover a lot in this book. All of the topics are important in a happy and healthy life, but none will matter if we don't build on a solid foundation. That's why chapter 1 begins here: your faith.

First, let me share a little about my faith journey.

I grew up in a Christian family and went to church every single Sunday, even though I often didn't want to go. Church wasn't that fun to me, and I never seemed to fit in with the rest of the kids. I remember sitting there twiddling my thumbs because I was bored and had no idea what the pastor was saying. What is a *new covenant*? What does *die to self* even mean? Why was Jesus always referred to as a *lamb*? Lamb sure does sound tasty though!

Religion or faith was something I never fully grasped as a kid. I understood that Jesus died for me, that there was a God in the sky who deeply loved me, and that I could pray to him when I needed something. But even as I tried to read my Bible, go to church, listen to Christian worship music, and be a good kid for my parents,

21

something never clicked. I didn't know how or why to follow God. I just knew I was supposed to because my parents instructed me to do it, and I saw them do it, along with my six older siblings. (Yes, six, you read that right!)

A piece of the puzzle seemed to be missing for me. I wanted to love God and know him, but I simply didn't know how to. I kept sinning, struggling, and feeling alone. I was convinced that I was the *only* young girl in the world who had a struggle with porn and lust (kicking this off early with my secrets), because I thought only guys struggled with that. And in my early twenties, seeking male attention and going to the bars almost every weekend to get drunk and make poor decisions was my destructive hobby.

I was afraid to reveal these deep, dark secrets to anyone because I thought they would judge me and unveil my hypocritical life. I would show up to church hungover and tired from the night before. My parents would ask me, "What did you do last night?" and I would respond with a short, sweet answer: "Just hung out with some friends." Not only was I an addict, but now I was a liar too. I was so afraid to disappoint my parents and tell the truth. *Confused* was definitely one way to describe me.

When I was twenty-five years old and still living in Los Angeles, I was going through that breakup I mentioned in the introduction. I was desperate for help and sought out a counselor, Kacey, who also happened to be my Bible study leader and mentor. I pulled up to Kacey's house for a counseling session feeling sad, confused, and upset at God because I had lost this relationship. I had reverted back to partying on the weekends and questioning if God was good. I sat down in sweet Kacey's chair, and she said to me, "What do you want to talk about today?"

I responded, "I'm not sure, to be honest."

"I know what we are talking about," Kacey said. "The Lord revealed something specific to me about you for today."

I began to nervously shake in my chair and sweat. I thought, *Oh, shoot . . . What did God tattle on me to Kacey?*

Kacey has a beautiful, intimate relationship with God that I've always admired. She hears from the Lord so clearly, and I strongly desired that. She whipped out this piece of paper and proceeded to slam it on the table. On the paper was a single bold word written across the top:

HYPOCRITE

Ouch . . . that really hurt, I thought.

The piece of paper had a diagram with two different masks on it—one mask worn with some people, and another mask with others. She said, "Jeanine, I think this is you. You're living a double life. To some people, you are this godly girl, and to others, you aren't at all. A godly man won't want to marry a girl living a double life." Well, that was a tough punch to the gut.

At first, I felt judged and condemned by her, because I really thought I wasn't. I was still going to church, occasionally reading my Bible, and meeting with girls to talk about some faith-related things. I sank lower in my chair, turned bright red, and welled up with tears out of pure embarrassment and shame. I wished so badly I could deny what she was saying, but the more I sat there in this painful moment and reflected on my life and choices, the more I knew she was right.

She told me, "You need to decide what you're going to do. Are you going to keep having one foot in with God and one foot in with the world? How long will you teeter this line? *You have to choose.*"

I felt so naked. Kacey had seen right through my crap and the front I tried to put up for so long. I began to weep. Not just a few tears, but a full-on sob session. I knew I was living a double life. I processed with her that day on how to change and what to do going forward, but that moment stuck with me forever. Never before had someone called me out so bluntly, but it was something I needed, something we all need.

From that day forward, I knew something had to change. This moment was the beginning of finding God for myself. Turning away from my destructive ways in exchange for the pursuit of godliness wasn't easy at first. But it got easier the more I did it, and the more I did it, the more I found God and freedom. On that day, I chose God. Not because my parents made me, but because I wanted to.

Does this hit home for you at all? Have you ever felt like a full-fledged hypocrite like me? Living one way for others and another for the rest? Or just not knowing how to fully pursue God, so you opt for unhealthier patterns instead. It's an exhausting feeling with nothing but discontentment and disappointment. Dancing on the line for both gives you dissatisfaction because you don't get the full benefits of either. All God wants to do is give us his full joy in him when we follow him, yet we continue to choose things that only give us momentary satisfaction. But take it from me, it's not worth it.

Or maybe, for you, it looks like this. You feel like giving up on any faith you have because you've been playing telephone with God for a while and he's just not answering your calls. You're trying hard in your own strength to connect with him, but it's not working. This can lead to disappointment, or even avoiding spending time with him or praying, because it feels like your time will be wasted. You may experience jealousy toward other Christians who *seem* to have it figured out when you don't.

I'm here to tell you, every Christian goes through these feelings, and no Christian has it all figured out. Take a deep breath and exhale the pressure to have it all together. I've been there many times in the trenches of my insecurities and fears, burying myself with guilt and performance to try to earn God's love, not knowing that I already have it. And so do you.

However you may feel toward God or currently in your faith journey, I want to gently remind you of this: you're not too far gone, too dirty, too broken, or too messed up to come back to God. *Don't let yesterday's mistakes stop you from making the right choices today.* Let me clear this up for you: God is not mad at you. God never desired for you to feel shame and guilt but rather joy and freedom. The enemy condemns and shames us, while God convicts and heals us. This is key to remember along this journey, because otherwise you will always think God is out to get you, when instead, he just wants to gently nudge you to come back to his loving arms where there is safety and protection.

As I mentioned at the beginning of this chapter, I decided to focus on faith first because if you don't get the foundation right, you'll build your house on quicksand. That house won't stand without Christ. I know many of you came to this book because you want answers that will help you in your dating life, friendships, career, fitness, and so much more. I promise you, we'll get there, but we have to start here. How do I know? Because I had it all backward. I thought all the wrong things would make me happy—the perfect guy, the hottest outfit, the "right" weight on the scale, the fanciest car, the right friends. But peace didn't come with any of that; rather, it was more exhaustion. It wasn't until the moment I stepped forward with Jesus that I truly found the answers to a fulfilling, meaningful life of purpose that I had been searching for my whole life.

My hunch is that there are people reading this who might have been hurt by their church, or are frustrated with God, or are simply skeptical of whether this whole God thing is real. I encourage you to have an open mind and receptive heart and allow God to speak to you throughout this book. He wants to give you a deeper revelation of himself, and I'm going to try to help you get there with these next couple of tips.

Surround Yourself with People Who Love and Know God

We are shaped by our surroundings. They will drastically dictate who we become and what we do. Take a look at your surroundings and ask yourself, *Is this a successful environment to help me become who I want to be?* Your surroundings can be where you hang out and who you hang out with. Are the people and environments you are around daily and weekly encouraging you to grow in your faith, commit to a church, speak life over yourself, read Scripture, and overall know and follow Jesus? If not, let's work on that.

I want to be careful that I'm not promoting legalism or more performance but rather daily disciplines that will spur you on in your faith. Overall, finding friends who walk consistently with God will be essential in your faith journey. We will talk more about this in the friendship chapter, but who you do life with will shape the trajectory of your life. This is what changed my life—changing my circle of people.

A great first step toward surrounding yourself with people who love and follow God is finding a church you connect with; show up consistently and meet with other believers. When you're struggling, those people will love on you, pray for you, and give you biblical advice. Try out a couple churches, put yourself out there, meet the pastor if you can, ask questions about the church, and stick with it. Give it six weeks before you decide to stay or try another one. Remember, there is no perfect church, but find one that you enjoy and can commit to. The main thing to look for: do they teach the Bible and live it out? If so, you're in a good spot!

Prioritize Your Time with God

Spending time with God is super important because it's how you gain a deeper connection with him and can hear his voice more, but sometimes it can feel a bit daunting. Where do you begin? What do you even do? How do you understand this big, complex book? One thing to remember is that your time with God is *your* time, so make it special and unique to you. It is not black and white. It does not have to be all cozy with candles, coffee, and music, like an Instagram influencer. But if you like that and it helps, do it! Find a setting and time every day, if possible, that encourages you to want to read undistracted. The main priority is just acknowledging God in your day and taking time to just be with him—whatever that may look like.

For me, my time with God doesn't always look magical, but I prioritize it because I understand the value in it. In the beginning of this chapter, I talked about how I didn't understand the Bible. My times with God felt empty because I didn't know:

- the value of the Bible and the power it could have over my life
- where to start in the Bible
- how to understand it
- how to make it a priority

Many attribute Charles Spurgeon or Vance Havner with saying, "A Bible that's falling apart usually belongs to someone who's not." No matter who said it, it's true. Once I began to read my Bible more, I found my life was less stressful, my thought life was less chaotic, and I knew God's voice more. Intaking the Word consistently will greatly benefit your life and decisions going forward.

THE JOHN 21-DAY CHALLENGE

If you're looking for a way to develop a habit of reading Scripture, try this.

It's commonly said that it takes twenty-one days to form a habit. Serendipitously, there are twenty-one chapters in the gospel of John.

In this challenge, read one chapter a day for twenty-one days.

From there, keep reading a chapter a day until you get to the end of the New Testament.

Many biblical teachers encourage new Bible readers to begin with John: it's a great place to begin for both new and longtime readers. It's a book of the Bible that vividly and beautifully humanizes Jesus, bringing his heart and character to life.

Tip: if you need another good book to jump to or read a verse a day from, check out Proverbs or Psalms.

BIBLE APPS

Here's a list of phone apps to help you understand what you're reading in the Bible:

1. Enduring Word Commentary
2. BibleProject
3. Read Scripture
4. Blue Letter Bible
5. Verse by Verse Ministry

TIPS FOR READING THE BIBLE

1. Pick a translation of the Bible that encourages you to read and understand. My favorite is the English Standard Version (ESV), which is known for its accuracy and readability. Other good options include the New Living Translation (NLT) and the Amplified Bible (AMP).
2. Pick a time of day for your reading that you can stick to. I like to read in the morning before I work out and start my workday.
3. Create an environment free from distractions like your phone or TV.
4. Pick a book in the Bible and read a verse or chapter a day. I read at least one chapter per day and underline words or lines that stand out.
5. While you read, take your time to process the meaning of the words and how they apply to you. Apps can also help with comprehension and application.
6. Journal a verse that spoke to you. Jot down a prayer, any thoughts, and what you feel like God is saying to you through his Word.
7. Pray at the beginning or the end that the Lord would reveal himself to you through his Word. Pray over what you and others need.
8. Optional: play worship music while you read to create a sense of calm. (I enjoy instrumental music by William Augusto.)

Reading and understanding the Bible is the best first step in your journey of becoming happy and healthy, because it is a guide for a more blessed life here on earth and eternally. If you read the Word and apply it to your life, your new life changes will already be off to an amazing start. Just you wait and see!

Consider What You Are Consuming

Weirdly enough, I love driving. I love jamming out to my music and trying to cut down the time to my destination like I'm in a video game. Anyone else? I wouldn't say I'm someone who has road rage, but there have been times when I've been enjoying my drive until someone cuts me off or does something I deem as "bad" driving, and what do I do? I get frustrated, yell, and might accidentally drop an f-bomb. *Oops, where did that come from?* I don't normally cuss—I actually try to avoid it—but what I fill my mind with is what is going to come out of my mouth. I notice that if I listen to more vulgar music, cuss words tend to fly out of my mouth more, and that's not really the look I want. Matthew 12:34 (ESV) says, "Out of the abundance of the heart the mouth speaks." After reading this, it's no wonder why that came out.

Did you know that the heart is responsible for pumping blood to every cell in your body? Your heart is a vital vessel that influences everything you do, which is why God places such an emphasis on guarding it and being careful what you put into it. It's like a compass that tells you where to go and what to do, so be mindful what you're feeding it, because that's what will flow out of it, as stated in Proverbs 4:23: "Above all else, guard your heart, for everything you do flows from it."

So what are you feeding it? Consider what TV shows, movies, music, social media, podcasts, and books you are consuming. We scroll on our Instagram "feeds" like we're consuming food. All of these are either positively or negatively affecting your spirit and mind, whether you like to admit it or not. They have subliminal and direct messages being fed to us, telling us how to view ourselves, love, sex, money, God, and life. So be on guard! Actions follow thoughts, and thoughts follow your mind. Feeding your mind God's biblical truths and uplifting worship music are a sure way to have a more fruitful life.

The Bible challenges us to focus and reflect on things differently than the world does. In Philippians 4:8 (emphasis added), the apostle Paul writes, "Finally, brothers and sisters, whatever is *true*, whatever is *noble*, whatever is *right*, whatever is *pure*, whatever is *lovely*, whatever is *admirable*—if anything is *excellent* or *praiseworthy*—think about such things." This list challenges us to keep our minds fixed on and filled with things that are only beneficial, God honoring, and good. Not only will it bless you, but it will bless others too. Take some time to meditate on this list.

29

A PLAYLIST FOR A HAPPY, HEALTHY MINDSET

Kari Jobe, "First Love"

Elevation Worship, "Forever YHWH"

Maverick City Church, "Promises"

Hillsong Worship, "Pursue/All I Need Is You"

Bethel Worship, "Back to Life"

Phil Wickham, "1,000 Names"

Upperroom, "Defender"

I pray as this chapter closes that first and foremost you don't leave condemned but encouraged. God is closer than you know. I hope you know how much Jesus loves you. He loves to help you in this journey. This isn't about performance or playing a game with God but rather having a real, intimate relationship with him. The more you experience his love for you, the more genuine change will happen. It's *out* of his love for us that repentance and obedience follow, not the other way around. Now you have to make a choice, just like I did. I pray you will take time after this chapter to sit with him, talk to him, and ask him to reveal himself to you on a deeper level. Make him your first love and watch what happens!

MAKE IT REAL IN YOUR LIFE

1. Do you believe God is who he says he is? If yes, why? If no, why not?
2. What is something holding you back from truly following God and going all in?
3. What is something you are consuming that you need to cut?
4. What first step can you start today in order to follow God?

2

Expectations

When You Feel You're Falling Behind

Ah, the infamous feeling of falling behind. You feel as if you're missing out on something, or that time is running out, or that you can't keep up with your peers' achievements. You want to celebrate others, yet it's hard because they have something you don't. You might think, *Why, God? Why does she get that and not me?* You thought by now you would be married, or have kids, or have a house, or have traveled more, or made a certain income, but the facts state otherwise, leaving you disappointed and discouraged. Maybe you've gotten so close to getting the very thing you wanted, but at the last minute it was ripped away from you. Life feels cruel and unfair. I know this feeling all too well. This chapter truly hits home for me as it's something I'm walking through right now.

As I write this, I'm twenty-eight years old and still single. All my friends are either already married, long-term dating someone, or getting engaged. Yet here I am alone in my home and wondering, *Am I meant to be single forever? Is something wrong with me? Do I have to celebrate* another *engagement?* It feels as if time is running out for good things to happen as my twenties close on me. And it doesn't help that I live in Dallas, aka the land of people getting married left and right within six months of meeting.

This season has held a very interesting dichotomy between being so challenging yet so exciting. I'm thrilled that I get to watch my best friends find the loves of their lives and get married, but I'm devastated that I'm just out of a serious relationship and back in the dating game again. I want to celebrate my friends, and I will, but sometimes I just can't help but feel like I'm falling behind or missing out on something I'm supposed to have.

How did I get here? This is *not* what I expected or signed up for. Why, God? Why me? Anyone else?

Although these feelings are difficult and valid, with time and maturity, I have grown to shift my perspective on life and let go of the expectations I have put on myself. That's my hope and prayer for you too by the end of this chapter.

My friend Holly, whom I met at a Christian women's camp two years ago, told me in May 2021, "Do not expect what you are expecting. God operates beyond our infinite minds." She was relating this to dating in particular, because I've always dated a certain type of guy. She suggested I try dating men who aren't traditionally my type, because the man she married was "unexpected and not who she normally goes for." But she shared that her marriage to him was the best relationship she's ever had. After a year, she and I talked once again, and she said something that really struck me. She said, "The unexpected doesn't mean less than," meaning that just because something is not what we expected or originally desired doesn't mean it can't still be good. *Oof, this got me.* I pondered that for a bit and felt that the Lord gave me a whole revelation based on this one sentence.

And this is my revelation:

Often, we create rigid timelines and unrealistic expectations of when we will have a house, when we will be married, when we will have kids, who we will marry, what he will look like, etc. You can fill in the blank of what that is for you. But we just want what we want, when we want it—and when we don't get it, we're left disappointed.

Unmet expectations lead to disappointments.[1] We boss God around and demand things from him—"I want to be married by twenty-four," "I expect a good job right out of college," "I want a big, white house in a great location with a pool and a picket fence!" We look to God as a vending machine or a magic genie, pleading for things. When we don't get what we want, we blame him and create distance from him. Dissatisfaction in life happens when God's solution doesn't match our expectation or our timelines. But we never even consulted God about the timeline in the first place.

Learning to Trust God's Timeline

Who says you are falling behind, anyway? Who even created these timelines? We did. Society did. Social media did. God certainly didn't create timelines or place these expectations on our lives. Social media plays a massive role in this, because when we endlessly scroll and see everyone else getting the one thing we want, we start to believe we're behind or failing. Or perhaps your parents are putting immense pressure on you to grow up, or get married, or get out of the house. Or maybe you're seeing everyone else in your friend group get to live your dream while it feels like you're sitting on the bench. I feel you, friend, I do.

The problem in comparing our timelines with others' is that we will either feel less than or greater than someone else by making them our measuring stick. We will either feel inferior or superior to them. Either envious or prideful, neither of which is God-glorifying. The only timeline you need to worry about is between you and God. He is where we will find true satisfaction, and he knows the perfect timing for it all. You are not too late or too early. You are right where God has you right now for a reason.

Where you live and who (or what) you surround yourself with can drastically determine how much you're aware of what you have or lack. Our surroundings and environment can massively dictate what we fixate on. This is worth noting, because if you live somewhere

where all people talk about is marriage, then you'll be more likely to stress about it, since it's a part of the culture there.

When I lived in California, people were super stressed about success and career. So naturally, I was too. I didn't really think about marriage and dating then; I was content being single. But as soon as I moved back to Dallas, I became fixated on relationships and marriage because it's a focus of so many conversations. Yes, we are shaped by our surroundings, but you have the power to choose *who* to surround yourself with and what thoughts you allow to run rampant. It's inevitable that culture will try to set the tone for your life, but ultimately, you get to decide if you will let culture dictate your life—or if you will let God do it. It may be beneficial to step out of your surroundings every now and then to shift your perspective and get a fresh one.

Who says you have to hit milestones for marriage, career, or anything else? When I open my Bible, I don't see God putting timelines on when people needed to have a baby, become king, get married, or begin their ministry. Heck, Sarah in the Bible desired a baby and didn't have one until she was ninety, and God still blessed and used her (Genesis 17:17, 21:2)!

What if you dropped your self-made timelines and expectations and stopped trying to force things to happen in your own timing because you don't trust God will come through? What if, yes, you made a goal or had a dream, but you prayed over it and then surrendered it to God for his timing and his will? What if your prayer became, "God, give me your will, your timing, and your plans—not mine." God wants to give you good things, and he's good at doing it too, but can you trust his timing with it? "If you then, who are evil, know how to give good gifts to your children, how much *more* will your Father who is in heaven give good things to those who ask him!" (Matthew 7:11 ESV, emphasis added). And we read in James, "Every good thing given and every perfect gift is from above, coming down from the Father of lights, with whom there is no variation or shifting shadow" (James 1:17 NASB).

I remember when I was in college, this girl in my sorority got engaged. We all stared at her perfectly shiny ring and screamed with joy for her, but deep down inside, I was filled with the green monster of envy. *It's not fair,* I thought. But looking back now, my life would be drastically different if I had gotten married my junior year of college. I probably wouldn't have accomplished the things I've done or traveled as much as I have if I had rushed God's timing out of a desire to be married. God has me right where he wants me, and he has the same for you. It may not be what or when you expected it, but it will be better when it's on God's timing.

Sometimes we can't recognize the good gifts he gives us because they are unfamiliar, unexpected, and not what *we* originally wanted. But it's in these moments that God shows us that he has so much more for us beyond our limited human perspective. Maybe the unexpected things we get are exactly what we needed all along to show us that we are not in control, but he is. Pray that when you get the good thing, you'll be able to recognize it's from God, even if it's not what you expected.

It's possible that the reason you don't have the very thing you want is because you're not supposed to—or at least not right now. I know that's hard to hear, but it's the truth. If you're measuring yourself by the world's timeline, you'll forever be behind. But if you let go of control over an idealized timeline, you'll forever be right on time. God's timing is perfect, and in it, patience and endurance are produced, which are essential to our faith. We may want things sooner or later, but God's plan for us is always right on time. When you trust and accept his timing, you'll be thankful you waited for it.

Waiting is hard, I know. But let me share with you something God revealed to me while I was waiting at the airport. I was sitting alone at a restaurant, waiting for my sister to come, since she was still stuck in security. Normally, when I sit alone and I know no one is coming to sit with me, I feel a bit anxious, lonely, and awkward. But this time was different. I was relaxed, calm, and expectant because I knew my sister was coming eventually. Even though there was an empty chair next to me, I knew with full confidence she would show up, so I waited differently. This is how it is with God. When you wait, knowing that even though you don't feel God next to you right now, you can still trust he will show up for you. It may look different from what you expected, but it will be better than you expected. It changes how you wait when you know God is with you and on your side.

This very thought has gone through my mind: *Why does* she *get this?*

And I get so many DMs from girls with the same question, because they are right there too.

Get this: I've been a bridesmaid in more than thirteen weddings. As I mentioned earlier, I desire to be the one with the white dress at the altar someday, with my forever guy at my side, but until then, I want to champion and celebrate my girlfriends as if it were my own day. You may wonder, how?

Celebrating Others When They Get What You Want

It all comes down to where our eyes are focused. We tend to feel like we are falling behind when we focus on others. We can become so consumed with other people's lives that we stop enjoying our own.

Imagine this: you finally bought your first house, the white one with the wraparound porch and cute little fence. You were so excited, but then your neighbor moves in. Here they come with a brand-new BMW, they put in a new pool and update the already flawless landscaping, and they have parties every weekend. You thought your house was nice and all, but then you looked over the fence into their yard and wondered, *Should I add a pool? Should I throw more parties? Do I need to drop more money, that I don't even have, to make my landscaping nicer?*

Suddenly you don't like your house anymore and feel like you don't have anything worth offering. Their house always seems better than yours. You become exhausted—or go broke—by trying to keep up. But what if instead of always looking at others' achievements

36

and possessions, you got busy focusing on what you *do* have instead of what you *don't*. You'd probably be a lot happier and less tired. But how can you go to your neighbor's house and watch them have all the things you want—and still celebrate them?

The ability to celebrate others getting the things we want comes with a lot of self-work. When I saw my best friend and roommate get engaged right after I went through a breakup, my heart shattered a little at first. For many months previously, she and I had sat for hours dreaming about our futures—whom we would marry, where we would move, what we would do with them, where we would travel with them, etc. For six months we were on the same path: both dating godly men with the hopes of marrying them. But our paths diverged as her relationship ended in an engagement and mine ended in a breakup. It was painful yet God-ordained.

Right after, many people asked me, "Are you okay? Do you feel jealous?" At first, I was. But eventually, with time, I could look people in the eyes with full honesty and say, "I am genuinely happy for her!" Was it hard? Yes. But is she easy to celebrate? Yes! And how did I get to that point? With honest journal entries, processing with trusted friends, and daily prayers asking God to help me surrender my own desires to him, I was able to fully celebrate my best friend when she got the very thing I've dreamt of since I was a kid.

Here are some things that I have clung to during this season that will hopefully help you too.

There is a season for everything

Season is an overused word, but it truly encapsulates one's current situation. Some seasons are fruitful and easy, and others are awful and challenging. I hope you aren't in the second season, but if you are, know that it won't last forever. I know it may feel hard right now, but these are the seasons that refine and shape us. I know this isn't the season you would have chosen for yourself, but God is still present in it and can still very much use it. In fact, he often allows seasons of lack or refinement to produce more fruit in us, because if we don't go through them, we may become complacent, idle, and too comfortable. Those times are usually when we push ourselves the most to grow, heal, deepen our relationship with God, and try new things.

We need these seasons for our overall betterment and growth! Each season is meant for a reason. We can look to Ecclesiastes 3 for what some of those seasons are:

> There is a time for everything,
> and a season for every activity under the heavens:
>
> a time to be born and a time to die,
> a time to plant and a time to uproot,
> a time to kill and a time to heal,
> a time to tear down and a time to build,
> a time to weep and a time to laugh,
> a time to mourn and a time to dance.
>
> Ecclesiastes 3:1–4

Sometimes God simply doesn't want us to have something because it isn't what we need at the moment—or at all—as painful as that may be to hear. But we have to trust that if he wanted us to have it, we would. If we don't have it, it's because he wants us to wait more or surrender the dream to him and let him bring other good things when he finds best. Regardless, in any season, you'll never go wrong by walking in full surrender to the Lord, because then you let go of your expectations and ask God for his best. Some seasons are absolutely necessary, because they will refine you and challenge you like no other time would, if you let them. Instead of asking God *Why?* ask him *What? What do you want to teach me through this, God?*

Reread that list in Ecclesiastes and identify your current season. This may be the very season you need right now to propel you into a better one, but you get to choose. *Will I let this season make me bitter or better?*

Celebrate others just as you would want to be celebrated

This may be the hardest part of this journey when you feel like you're falling behind, and it will take self-work and internal pep talks.

In Romans 12:15 (ESV), Paul says, "Rejoice with those who rejoice, weep with those who weep." Not only do you have a season you're going through, but so do others. It's important to remember that and to be there for people in both times. Truly rejoicing with others as they rejoice is a beautiful thing! It personally took me time—as well as overcoming insecurities and self-doubt—to get there, but once I did, I could genuinely look at someone and say, "I am so happy for you!" no matter what I was experiencing in my own season.

Often, we are too busy looking at ourselves and what *we* want that we forget to look to others and see what they need. We become so self-focused and self-consumed that all we think about are *our* desires and dreams, even to the point that we stop caring about others. And when they get the very thing you want, you can't help but be envious and bitter because you've thought about it for so long. Instead of getting bitter, flip the script. Ask others what they need and say, "How can I help you? How can I pray for you?"

Here's the thing: everyone wants to be seen, understood, and congratulated when they experience something wonderful. I know you would want that too when it's your turn to rejoice! You'd want everyone to come over, bring balloons and a cake, take pictures, and cheer you on! But can you do that for others? Can you celebrate others as you would want to be celebrated? It's easy to receive it, but can you give it? A true friend genuinely cheers when someone gets something they want, without resentment or jealousy.

It's something worth fighting for and deeply working on. It might require some pride being let down, but pride is something you'll want to try to remove from your life anyway. It might require remembering what the Bible says about being a good friend: "A friend loves at all times, and a brother is born for a time of adversity" (Proverbs 17:17).

It will require remembering who God says you are, how he loves you, and that he has good things for you, even if you don't see them right now. It might require processing your vulnerable feelings with a counselor or a trusted friend and asking them to speak truth back over you. It might require you to journal through your feelings of disappointment, as well as jotting all the ways God *has* moved in your life. And it might require you telling your friend that you are happy for them, and then going home and crying and praying through the feelings to God—because let's be honest, this may happen.

Finally, remember this: just because they got something good doesn't mean there's nothing good left for you. God isn't a God of lack or famine but a God of abundance.

Their timeline is not your timeline

This might be the most humbling part: realizing that someone else's journey is not yours.

You have been given a precious life, unlike any other who has ever walked this earth. Now, how will you steward it? You are a completely separate entity from anyone else: different DNA, parents, talents, abilities, lifestyle, background. There is not a one-size-fits-all approach for life. And that's amazing! How boring would it be if *all* our lives looked exactly the same? What if we all had the same job, same lifestyle, same interests, and got married around the same time? Would be kind of bland, right?

So often we try to play catch-up with one another, or even worse, compete with others, trying to reach those arbitrary milestones first. But the reason I'm able to stay optimistic is that I know God designed each of us uniquely with our own stories and timelines. Ephesians 2:10 (NABRE) says, "For we are his handiwork, created in Christ Jesus for the good works that God has prepared in advance, that we should live in them." God is a creator and a designer who designs everything intentionally. God makes each one of us different and loves each one of us intimately and uniquely.

40

He is writing a different story for you than he is for someone else. It may not be what you originally anticipated, but remember, God is in the unexpected, so your unexpected path can still be so purposeful. Proverbs 16:9 (ESV) says, "The heart of man plans his way, but the LORD establishes his steps." The journey God created for you is beautiful because no matter how much we try to mess it up, he can always find a way to restore it and correct it when we walk obediently with him.

I also want you to remember that the grass isn't always greener on the other side of the fence; it's green where you water it. And just because someone else's grass is green doesn't mean their home is peaceful. This is not to make you feel better about yourself because someone else may have it worse, but it's to remind you that things you see on social media are not always what they seem. We sit there scrolling and comparing our lives to other people's while not knowing what's really going on behind the scenes. Everyone has their own sin, struggles, brokenness, childhood trauma, and problems. We were never meant to find full satisfaction in earthly things anyway. Only God can truly bring us full joy and satisfaction; everything else is temporary and fleeting.

If your friend gets the thing you wanted and it goes south, this is not the time to secretly be happy. This is a time to go back to the earlier questions I proposed: "How can I help? How can I pray for you?" Rejoice when they rejoice, and mourn when they mourn. It's what good friends do.

As I close out this chapter, my prayer is that you feel less alone; more people feel this way than you can imagine. Trust me, if you saw my Instagram DMs, you'd feel the solidarity. Friend, I know this life isn't easy. I wish I could take away the pain from you. I wish I could hug you while you cry. But this season is temporary. I pray that you can look at yourself in the mirror and believe that God genuinely has the best for you. Next time you feel sad, jealous, or like you are falling behind, remember that you are right where you need to be. God isn't finished producing a work in you right where you are.

This journey may not be easy at times, but at least we're on one! We are now one step closer in the right direction of becoming happy and healthy. Let's do this!

MAKE IT REAL IN YOUR LIFE

1. Who are you comparing yourself to and why?
2. What about them do you admire, and if it's something honorable, how can you work toward that in your own way too?
3. What are you struggling to trust God with?
4. What self-made timeline did you create that you need to give to God?

3

Contentment

How to Keep Your Joy, Even When You're Alone

It was January 28, 2019, as I sat on my kitchen island for the first time in my new one-bedroom apartment in LA. I took a deep breath and looked at all the boxes of my belongings lying everywhere, and I let out a sigh. *I can do this*, I thought to myself. This was not exactly what I hoped for at this point in my life. I thought I would be living in a big, fun house with all my best friends in Los Angeles, but instead, here I was . . . all alone. The sun began to set and darkness set in.

With the darkness came an eerie feeling of knowing that I was completely alone. After previously living alone in college and going through a traumatic breakup (which I will share later), I vowed to myself that I would *never* live alone again, yet here I was—twenty-five, in a six-hundred-square-foot apartment in a new-to-me city. No one to come home to, say good-night to, talk to, cook with, or process all my fears with. Living alone is often a huge milestone for people. *I should be excited, right?*

Well, *excitement* isn't exactly how I would describe my emotions at that moment. More like *loneliness, fear, anxiety, confusion, worry*. Not only was I processing a new move, in a new city, but I had also just started a long-distance relationship at the same time I was having a painful falling out with a longtime best friend. It was a hard season with a lot of change happening all at once. I tried to find roommates, but everyone else already had their plans.

Before moving and picking this apartment, I had my mind made up to never live alone again, but right in the middle of telling God my plan and how it would be, my friend Sarah randomly texted me and said, "I feel like God wants me to tell you that he wants you to live alone. There's something special that he wants to do in this next season that will take you deeper with him."

I'm sorry, what? I am not doing that! I thought to myself. I was caught off guard by her words. I was fighting God's plan, but unexpectedly I felt God's peace in that moment. That text gave me the ultimate push to start looking at one-bedroom apartments. It was what I needed to let go of my plans and pursue God's. Admitting my fears, I surrendered my will and uttered the words, "Okay, God, I trust you. Do what you want." And he sure did! I lived alone for not only one year, but two. In those two years, I was refined, humbled, and learned how to have true intimacy in the Lord. I fell in love with God all over again. Plus, I even learned how to like myself!

I had no idea that living alone and learning to be alone would be so life-changing. I finally learned how to sit in God's presence; to enjoy going on adventures by myself (surfing, biking to the ocean at sunset, solo coffee shop dates, and hammocking at the park); to not rely on others for all my needs; and most important, to lean on God daily and realize I'm never actually alone. Amid many challenges, breakups, fears, and insecurities, I learned so much about myself—everything from forming my perfect morning routine to realizing unhealthy ways I used to cope. And most important, I learned how to trust God when my life doesn't look like what I thought it would and how to be confident being alone. That's my goal and prayer for you too.

Being in solitude can be scary because you can no longer run away from your haunting thoughts, past, or fears, plus it can bring out insecurities, questions about yourself, more loneliness, or doubts about whether you actually have dependable friends. For some people, isolation is uncomfortable because the constant noise, conversations, busyness, and other distractions that helped you cope and avoid suppressed feelings before are now gone. On the other hand, some people actually like being alone, maybe a little too much, since this is where you can hide who you are, avoid conflict, or ignore any true feelings. I'm not sure which category you find yourself in, but I do know God wants to meet you wherever you're at.

Being alone may be necessary for a season; however, we weren't meant to stay there. God designed us to be in community. It's important to have people help us carry our burdens, cry with us, laugh with us, and refine us. We'll talk about friendship and community in the next chapter because it matters!

The Secret Place with You and God

Why is being alone good? If we look to Scripture (bolded sections below are my emphasis), we see that Jesus went off to be alone often.

"Jesus often withdrew to **lonely places** and prayed" (Luke 5:16).

"In these days he went **out to the mountain to pray**, and all night he continued in prayer to God" (Luke 6:12 ESV).

"He withdrew from there in a boat to a desolate place **by himself**" (Matthew 14:13 ESV).

"After He had sent the crowds away, He went up on the mountain **by Himself** to pray; and when it was evening, **He was there alone**" (Matthew 14:23 NASB).

"Very early in the morning, while it was still dark, Jesus got up, left the house and went off to a **solitary** place, where he prayed" (Mark 1:35).

What are these verses trying to tell us?

There is something important and vital about being alone—and not only being alone, but being alone with God and drawing near to him. There's something about being alone with him that creates a bond like no other. It can only be generated by taking one-on-one time and space with God. In that unique time and space, he will speak to you, teach you, and help you grow.

Jesus didn't withdraw into solitude just for funsies. He didn't spend more than a month alone in the desert because he wanted to starve and be tempted by Satan for forty days just to see if he could do it. Spoiler alert: he could! He went away with an *intention*: to create deeper *intimacy* with his Father. His fulfillment had to come first from his Father before he could pour into others. His alone time mattered. And so does yours.

This is what I like to call *the secret place*. It's a place for just you and God. This place creates genuine intimacy with God. Matthew 6:6 (ESV) says, "But when you pray, go into your room and shut the door and pray to your Father who is in secret. And your Father who sees in secret will reward you."

The secret place matters because it's where no one else can affirm your actions and praise you for them; it's only between you and God. The Bible verse you post on Instagram, wearing a cross necklace, leading that small group at church—these are all good things, but they must come from a pure, genuine place after seeking God in private first. In the secret place, you have an audience of one: God. The only one who really matters. And God will bless you when you steward this time well and seek to draw near to him, revealing truth that you might not have seen otherwise. It's easy to pray in front of people and put on a show, but to really sit alone with God and be your authentic self is quite difficult.

Try this 5:5:5 method to begin: five minutes of reading your Bible, five minutes of journaling your thoughts and prayers, and five minutes of praying or sitting in silence with God.

That's fifteen minutes a day! Eventually, you may realize you want to spend more time than this, but start small if you need to. Small choices lead to big changes! When I first lived alone, this was the hardest thing for me. I was often distracted and rushed when I tried to read my Bible or pray. I couldn't silence my mind, but with consistent practice, it became a part of my routine.

God is always speaking, but we are often not listening. We are so busy scrolling, talking, planning, and rushing around that we cannot hear his voice. To gain more intimacy with God, we must slow down, silence outside distractions, and work on our self-discipline. For me, my distraction is my phone. So whatever your distraction may be, try removing it from your environment or go somewhere that doesn't have it.

Even though I was scared to live alone in the beginning, my friend was right—the Lord did want to do something special with me in my quiet, deeper intimacy with him. It held some of the most rewarding times with the Lord that prepared me for many other seasons in my life. Preparation for bigger moments is formed in the private moments with the Lord.

Solo Adventures

After going through a breakup with the guy I was dating long-distance, I was facing a lot of disappointment and discouragement, and sulking anxiously alone in my home sure didn't help, so I decided it was time for a road trip. By myself. *Wish me luck.*

As I began to look at places I could travel to for the weekend, I got nervous. I'd never done this before in my life. Looking at Google maps, I checked out all the beach towns within driving distance. When I landed on Santa Barbara, a two-hour drive from my home, I booked the cutest, quaintest little rental by the beach and set off on my journey. I loaded up my car with my surfboard, a weekend bag, my pillows, some snacks, a speaker, beach towel, my journal, Bible, and some books—and I was ready to go!

As I began that road trip, I was overwhelmed with excitement and joy. But the more I drove and sat alone in my thoughts, the sadder and more nervous I got. As I sat alone in my car for two plus hours, I was forced to face so many feelings I had been avoiding. *Why is this so hard? Is there something wrong with me? Why did God make me single again?* Once I arrived and saw the ocean and beautiful town, my excitement came rushing back. I checked into my rental and felt ready to take on the weekend.

Over the next three days, I prayed more than I had in a long time. I went to the beach and sat there in silence, inviting God to speak to me. I read chapters and chapters of Scripture, letting it wash over me and renew me. I went shopping by myself, got lunch by myself, cooked while listening to worship music, went surfing in a new spot, and called some friends along the way. Next thing I knew, I was enjoying this solo getaway! But it didn't come easy at first. I had to battle the thoughts of feeling uncomfortable, lonely, awkward, and thinking people were looking at me wondering, *Why is she eating alone?* But I realized, once my perspective about it changed, so did the outcome of the trip. When I stopped caring what other people thought about me, I was able to enjoy where I was and what I was doing. I was able to experience God in a way I hadn't in a long time. I was able to experience the contentment and wholeness I had been longing for.

PACK FOR A HAPPY, HEALTHY SOLO WEEKEND ADVENTURE

1. Bible
2. Journal and pen
3. Speaker
4. Blanket or hammock to sit outside
5. Comfy walking shoes
6. Accessories for the weather (sunglasses, sweater, hat)
7. Snacks
8. Book
9. Water bottle
10. Positive mindset

Don't shy away from making bold, unusual decisions because you're more concerned about what people think than what amazing thing could happen! We may be nervous that people think we are weird for doing something a bit different, but letting people dictate your decisions can prevent you from following God's voice. If you know something is from God or would lead you closer to God, follow his voice, not people's. We'll talk about this more in chapter 8.

I want to challenge you to try to go somewhere new by yourself, regardless of the discomfort. You could make yourself a picnic and go to a park, go to a movie alone, go to a museum, sit by a lake with a hammock and read, or sit at a restaurant and treat yourself to a nice meal! Date yourself, essentially! If you are single, do things you'd like to do or go places you'd like to go with a partner! Even if you are dating or married, I still encourage you not to lose this.

TAKE YOURSELF ON A DATE CHALLENGE

1. Pick a date
2. Pick something new you'd love to try
3. Get dressed up cute
4. Put your favorite makeup on
5. Try to meet someone new
6. Journal through your experience and thoughts after

Enjoying time alone is useful no matter what season you're in. If this all feels too much, start smaller, like visiting a coffee shop alone. People often go to coffee shops by themselves. Bring your journal, Bible, or a good book, get your music going, and enjoy time getting to know yourself. Sit in silence with yourself. Let yourself feel thoughts you've been running from for a while. Pause and take a deep breath. Journal through your feelings or fears. Give God space to speak to you. The more you do this, the easier it becomes. And who knows, maybe the next thing you do is take a solo weekend trip and spend intentional time with just you and God.

Being alone with God is meant to be a safe space. When you're alone, you're forced to depend on him and him alone. No one else is watching; no one else is there to judge or distract you. Scream, cry, lie on your floor, say out loud what you are truly feeling, and come as you are. Don't run to God as a last resort, but run to him daily, in everything. Watch how much your relationship deepens with him the more you do this!

Solitude Versus Isolation

We've talked about the benefits of being in solitude with the Lord, but what about the negatives? Being alone with God is never a bad thing, but being alone too much and letting time alone turn into isolation can be harmful. Isolation is when you purposely separate yourself from others in order to run or hide from someone or something. Isolation turns into a dangerous place because it's where you have no one to help you if you are struggling. The Bible is very clear about this: "Two are better than one, because they have a good return for their labor: If either of them falls down, one can help the other up. But pity anyone who falls and has no one to help them up" (Ecclesiastes 4:9–10) and "A person standing alone can be attacked and defeated, but two can stand back-to-back and conquer. Three are even better, for a triple-braided cord is not easily broken" (Ecclesiastes 4:12 NLT).

God knows we are more susceptible to temptation when we are alone. We increase the chances of resisting the enemy by being around people who can offer wise counsel and pray with us. In Luke 8:26–39, we read about a man who was demon possessed. Demons had driven him into *solitary* places. Why is this? Because the enemy knows he has more leverage to speak lies to you when you have no one to help you combat them. He knows strength is found in numbers, so when someone is alone and weak, he targets them and tries to keep them there. The enemy will always push us toward isolation, which inevitably leads to loneliness, confusion, and poor decision-making. God, on the other hand, wants us to master the art of solitude, not isolation. *Solitude draws you near to God; isolation pushes you away.*

Solitude usually connects you to the Lord in intimacy, but isolation disconnects you from everything good—including your relationship with the Lord and others.

I once heard a pastor named Jonathan Pokluda speak about this. He said, "Every idea seems like a good idea in isolation."[1] I've found this to be true in my own life. The times I'm isolated—separated from people while also not connecting with the Lord—are always the times I've fallen into temptation and made unwise decisions. Once, when I was lonely and bored, I went on a random Hinge date, and let's just say . . . it did *not* go well. He was on his phone half the time, he kept asking me about my ex, and then he admitted to being in rehab for alcohol, which I'm not against, but I'd prefer someone who has healed from that addiction already. Overall, it was just awkward and *not* it. I kindly asked him to bring me home because I was not feeling it and didn't see us moving forward. If I had just had a friend ask me some questions before going and process with me my intentions of why I was going on the date, it probably would have spared me that uncomfortable experience.

Proverbs 18:1 (ESV) says, "Whoever isolates himself seeks his own desire; he breaks out against all sound judgment." Isolation causes weakened judgment. You are more inclined to struggle or make an unwise decision in isolation. Wisdom would be reaching out to a friend, a parent, a teacher, a leader, or a mentor and asking for advice and insight. I sure wish I had!

You might wonder, *What if I like being alone more than with people?* That's a valid question. God has wired each of us differently. Some of us crave alone time because it's how we refresh ourselves, while others are energized by being around people. I am not suggesting you ignore your natural inclination, but I am encouraging you to note where you are naturally swayed and challenge yourself to healthily push yourself out of your normal routine sometimes. I like to have my mornings alone with God and refuel myself with people at night. Find a good routine for yourself, but never forsake good quality time with the Lord, no matter what.

Single and Secure

It would be a miss to finish this chapter without touching upon singleness. While not everyone reading this book may be single, it may still speak to you. Let's talk about singleness and being secure in that. Maybe you cringed just reading that word! For some people, being single is something you might look at like it's a disease or a curse, but I see it as a blessing. It might be cliché or annoying to say, but hear me out.

I think singleness is truly one of the best gifts and seasons in your life. Learning to be secure in your individuality apart from someone else will *always* be beneficial. Singleness isn't just about a lack of relationship with someone else but about your relationship with yourself. Being alone and confident applies to singleness because being secure in your singleness will help you be secure in your relationships. The more you are stable and rooted in Christ for your identity and security, the less you'll need it from others. I get a lot of DMs from girls who feel broken or unwanted because of their singleness. If that's you, then this section is for you, my friend.

The incredible apostle Paul tells us in 1 Corinthians 7 that it is better to be single than married—*who would have thought?* I know culture doesn't push that message too often, but Paul says the married people's interests are divided between each other, the world, and God, while the single person gets to devote themselves wholeheartedly to the Lord. He says it is better for them to remain unmarried. Why? Because you get to focus on just you and God and your mission with him. You and God are a complete item. Nothing and no one else has to come in to fulfill the rest. I know that may not be what you want to hear, but when someone else comes into the picture, your focus and commitments will inevitably shift a bit.

This is the time to grow in the Lord, learn more about yourself, try new things, go on trips, say yes to new adventures, move abroad, or whatever else you want to do! If you get into a relationship and eventually become married, your life will not look the same anymore. It's not a bad thing, it will just be different. Every decision—from the job you take or a trip you plan, to what you eat for dinner or where you go to church—has to now consider that other person. You don't have to do that when you're single, so you are free to fully follow God and live your own life. You might be able to do these things with your partner, but why not start them now and not wait for another person for life to begin?

Singleness doesn't have to feel like a curse if you view it as an investment opportunity instead. Investment can look like falling deeply in love with God, getting yourself healthy, healing from any childhood wounds or past hurts, going to counseling, moving to a new city, knowing what you like and don't like, and becoming more secure and confident in yourself. When you invest in yourself, you'll see this be rewarded well into your future. Healthy single people make healthy married couples. The healthier both you and your partner are individually, the healthier you will be collectively. If singleness is done well, it may actually be harder to give up because you've become so content with yourself and God.

If singleness has been extremely difficult for you, please know you're not alone. I know the feeling. During one long season of singleness where I just wanted to be in a relationship, I went on unnecessary dates, resented God, questioned my self-worth, and felt like something was wrong with me. Have you felt that before too? When you're single, you may feel like you're in the wilderness of no good options or failed talking stages; like no matter how hard you try, it doesn't work out. Here's a solution: stop trying.

Okay, hold up. I'm not saying to hide in your house and expect God to drop someone through the chimney, but I am saying to surrender to God your singleness and your desire to be married. Don't try to force it in your own strength. Of course, say yes to dates if you'd like to go, and be an active part of a church community where you may meet more potential contenders, but don't try to rush God's timing, because then it's not God's timing anymore.

People want to rush to the altar to solve a feeling of loneliness or incompleteness, but another person was never meant to solve those for us. Only God was. To avoid codependency on a person, where you make them your entire world, try to use singleness as a time to work out many of your insecurities and feelings of dependency. Make the best of it! One day if you're married, I think you'll look back and thank your single self for using the season well. It can be as good as you want to make it.

Singleness will be in seasons for most people, so while you have it, shift your perspective to see it as a gift and something that you should cherish while you have it. If later you get the gift of marriage, you can cherish that season as well. Later we will talk about dating and relationships, but I wrote this chapter first because I think it will help you in your romantic relationships. I hope you can shift your perspective in this time to see it as something beneficial and a blessing.

My prayer is that you now understand why being alone with God matters so much. If the Savior of the world went away often to pray and meet with his Father, then I pray we emulate Jesus and make it a regular part of our routine to do the same. Challenge yourself to be okay with not feeling fully okay sometimes. It's okay if it's uncomfortable. It's okay if you feel uncertain or awkward sometimes. It's okay if you don't have it all figured out right now. God is not done yet. He's still working on you for his good. In the long run, your future self will thank you when you can spend a whole day alone and absolutely own it. You got this, friend!

MAKE IT REAL IN YOUR LIFE

1. Does being alone scare you? If so, why?
2. How will you be intentional about spending more alone time with God?
3. Are you running away from a feeling by avoiding being alone? If so, what?
4. How will you challenge yourself to practice dating yourself?
5. How will you use your singleness for good and for God?

Friendships

How to Have Healthy Ones That Last

I remember walking around my college campus as a tear trickled down my cheek, thinking, *I don't fit in here and no one cares about me.* I looked around, and it seemed like everyone else had friends but me. The sorority girls had their matching shirts and walked to class together while laughing; the athletes strutted together and bonded over their shared love of a sport; and many others I saw had people to eat lunch with, go to fun events with, and study with. Meanwhile, here I was on a campus of fifty thousand people, feeling lonelier than ever. I slowly shuffled my feet around, put my sunglasses on to cover my puffy eyes, and increased the volume to my sad girl Lana Del Rey music.

After six months of feeling like this, I finally decided to try to fix it (keyword *try*). I joined my college's competitive cheerleading team and Christian sorority, thinking that joining these groups would solve all my friend problems. But it turns out, it only created more. As I began to hang more with my cheer friends, who all liked to party, suddenly I began to party too. I had never partied before, so alcohol was new and intimidating for me. Slowly but surely, I began to get accustomed to it. But even though I was in a Christian sorority at the same time, I still struggled to feel fully known and like I fit in.

I dropped out of my sorority after only one semester, partly due to my YouTube channel consuming more time than I had expected. Trying to manage the logistics of my unexpected success, on top of trying to manage (or ignore) my feelings of shame and hypocrisy about my partying, I separated myself from that Christian community. Instead of leaning into relationships with like-minded believers, I ran away—and toward a much different lifestyle.

I began to hang out with only my cheerleading friends. Next thing I knew, I was fully living a life that didn't reflect Christ anymore. Partying on the weekends, looking for the next guy to make out with, and the next day going to church hungover (or not at all), all while some of my grades were declining. This became my cycle for most of college and post college. It was quite unfulfilling. I thought that I was living my best life, but in reality, I was creating a life of regret.

This all changed for me when I moved to California and found a Bible study at my church. There, I found my best friends, who actually challenged me and helped me grow into someone who looks more like Jesus. I had no idea that my friends and circle would make such an impact on my life in college. I wish younger me had known that. I wish younger me knew that who you surround yourself with is who you become, so choose wisely. It sure would have helped me make better choices about who I hung out with.

I'm not sure where you are on your journey of friendships, but I know this is genuinely one of the most difficult things to figure out in our young adult years. One of my most listened to episodes of my podcast *Happy and Healthy* is the one where I talk about friendships. Seems like people need community—and badly. Loneliness and isolation are increasing, while deep, healthy relationships are decreasing. And social media isn't helping that. More people than ever are opting for isolation and living alone. We are the generation of *over* "protecting our peace" to the point of removing all people who minorly inconvenience us, leaving us isolated and lonely.

Most people don't even know where to find friends or how to maintain healthy friendships. I believe this theme of friendship is by far one of the most make-or-break aspects in our lives, and I believe there is hope for this situation!

The Bible is clear about the importance of surrounding yourself with good people—and not just good people, but godly people. What does the Bible say about friendship?

> "Bad company corrupts good morals" (1 Corinthians 15:33 NASB).
> "Whoever walks with the wise becomes wise, but the companion of fools will suffer harm" (Proverbs 13:20 ESV).
> "The righteous choose their friends carefully, but the way of the wicked leads them astray" (Proverbs 12:26).

The Bible explains how people can build us up with encouragement, refine us with correction, help us when we are weak, and simply provide companionship as we walk through the everyday moments of life. Ecclesiastes 4:9 tells us, "Two are better than one." My life changed when I changed my playmates and my playgrounds, aka who I hung out with and where I hung out with them. Finding community doesn't come easy, but it's absolutely something worth fighting for. So how do we do it?

Finding Friends

One of the most commonly asked questions I get on social media is, "How do I find friends?" Understandably so! If you don't already have friends established from childhood, high school, or college, finding new ones can be increasingly difficult, especially as we get older. Finding friends is going to require effort. Unfortunately, friends will not magically appear at your front door, sorry! You are going to need to participate with God on this one.

When I lived in California, I was ready to grow more in my faith and knew I couldn't do it alone. I began to seek out Christian community. It was a bit difficult. One day I prayed, "God, if you don't bring me a Bible study, I will create one myself." I was prepared to partner with God to take the necessary steps required to find community. As I continued to pray, I randomly met a girl at a house gathering who happened to have just started a small group through our church, and she invited me. It was an answered prayer! I began to meet every single week with this group, and it genuinely changed my life.

Here's what I learned from that experience: you have to be willing to go out of your way and step out of your comfort zone to find new friends. When I met that girl, I didn't know anyone at the party besides two people, but I was willing to go and meet new people. New potential friends could be right under your nose! People you see at the gym, people who work at your local coffee shop, your neighbors, people you often see at the grocery store, people on social media, and especially people at your local church could all be your next potential friends! Sometimes people just need you to make the first move to initiate a friendship. This could simply look like, "Wow, I love your dress! I'm Jeanine, by the way. Nice to meet you! Where are you from?" Then let the conversation flow from there. It doesn't have to be weird or forced. Being kind and complimentary go a long way!

Finding friends may look like disrupting your normal routine to try something new. It might mean you move to a new city in an effort to find more life-giving people. I know several people who moved to Dallas specifically because of how well people do friendship here. A best friend of mine called me one day crying because she felt so lonely. The current friends she had were not uplifting her and were actually pulling her down. We prayed and prayed, and she decided to switch up which church service she went to and joined a new women's group at the church. One day she texted me, saying, "Jeanine, God showed up today! I asked for a new godly community, and I just met a group of ten women at the 9:30 service. Things are changing! Prayers work!" That was the best feeling to hear! This goes to show you that we should pray and ask God for people, but also be willing to try new things and put ourselves out there. The local church is often the best place for anyone to find community. That's one of the goals of the local church, after all—to connect the body of Christ together so we do not suffer alone.

So, I'm challenging you: try something new! Join a new church, a small group, a new sports league or workout class, or a group online that meets up weekly for people in your city—or even make the leap and move somewhere new! You'll never know until you try.

How to Look For and Be a Good Friend

Once you're meeting people and putting yourself out there, you need to ask a couple questions. First, what should I be looking for in a friend? And second, what does it look like to be a good friend? After all, it's unfair to expect people to be something for you that you aren't willing to be for them. Friendships also take time.

Here are some things to look for in a friend and also strive to be yourself:

Honest

An honest friend will lovingly tell you the truth, even when you don't want to hear it. You're looking for someone who doesn't lie or exaggerate to make themselves seem better. A healthy friendship between two honest people makes room for healthy conflict that helps you become a better person and live up to your full potential.

Encouraging

A good friend will encourage you when you're feeling down or insecure. This person sees the best in you, even when you don't. They will kindly affirm the good qualities in you and will pray for you on a hard day. Someone who supports you when you get a new job, a raise, a new relationship, or a new house. Someone who is excited for you and wants to celebrate you. They will champion you, even if it's not something they have.

Reliable

You need someone you can trust to be there for you through thick and thin. Reliable friends aren't the kind of people who are only available when things are good but disappear when life gets hard. They show up when they say they will and stick with you when challenges arise.

Trustworthy

A good friend is someone you can tell anything to and trust they won't go tell everyone else all your problems. Typically, if someone talks badly about others to you all the time, they're probably gossiping about you too. So heed my warning. You want someone you can trust to have the best intentions for you and have your back even when you're not around.

Intentional

A good friend pays attention. They remember the little details about you—following up when you say you need prayer for something, sending you chocolate or flowers after a breakup, or bringing you medicine when you're feeling sick.

Godly

Most important, when you're looking for a friend, look for someone who loves God. Someone who walks with Christ, strives to look more like him, and will always push you back to Christ and ask, "What does God think about that?" A godly friend will pray for you, share Scripture with you, and will never encourage you to dabble in sin. Friendship always takes work, but it goes a lot smoother when two people love God first and then love each other the way God calls us to.

Hopefully this list gives you a good baseline of what to look for and be. Of course, no one is perfect and will do all these things flawlessly, but they are good characteristics to aim for and work toward. My best friends have almost all of these qualities, and I can tell you from experiencing the opposite that this creates easier and more life-giving friendships.

How to Do Daily Life with Friends

If you already have good friends, you're off to a good start! But I want to challenge you to go deeper. Friendships should make you a better person and sharpen you. Proverbs 27:17 says, "As iron sharpens iron, so one person sharpens another." I've seen so many people be complacent in their friendships because it's uncomfortable to ask the hard questions or have the tough conversations, but in reality, all healthy friendships will require them. Friendships should be more than just getting dinner, going to group hangouts, or seeing the newest movie in theaters.

Deep friendships require effort and consistency. It's asking, "How are you? No, how are you *really*?" and often. It's sitting on the couch, holding your friend, and crying with her after a breakup. It's writing letters of encouragement when they are feeling less than, or sending funny TikToks when they need a pick-me-up. It's picking up their grocery order or walking their dog when they're feeling overwhelmed. It's checking up on your friend when you know they're struggling or shifting into isolation, and grieving with them after they go through a loss. It's sitting with them not only during the highs but in the non-Instagrammable lows too. It's knowing someone deeply—and allowing them to know you that well too—so you can genuinely help each other through hard seasons and point each other to God through it all.

This type of friendship requires intentionality, honesty, and vulnerability, and that courageous authenticity is a good litmus test for true friendship. Commit to spending regular time together—taking walks, studying together at the coffee shop, working out, hosting a party together, reading a book or the Bible together, or even planning a weekend getaway together. And commit to being open and digging deep. Praying for one another. Asking each other questions, often. Stay curious about your friend, and know what and who shaped them into who they are today. Everyone has a story; most people just don't ask about it. Let's be people who are intentional about learning someone's story and making them feel seen, safe, and known.

Friendships will have ebbs and flows, but all friendships require two people putting in time and effort, and sometimes one more than the other during busy seasons. Your friendships should challenge you and help you look more like Jesus. They should bring out the best in you (and you should do the same for them). Surround yourself with people who call you higher and push you back to Christ, even when it's hard. This is how true friendships are formed.

Toxic Friends

The word *toxic* has become quite a buzzword. We list everyone and everything unpleasant or challenging as toxic now. Yes, some people are truly toxic, but most toxic people just have an inner child that is deeply hurt and unhealed. I am not saying this to justify their actions but to encourage you to pay attention, look deeper, and try to figure out why people behave the way they do. Usually, these people have insecurities or unhealed wounds, so they bleed on people who never even cut them. This is why healing is so important! We'll talk more about this in later chapters, but typically, these types of people are anything but life-giving—they're life-sucking.

I've seen this in my own life. Regardless of how much time and effort I put into a friendship, if my friend or I are not healthy, the relationship will inevitably be unhealthy. Unhealthy friendships are unfortunately part of life. And let's admit it; sometimes we're the toxic friend. But no matter which friend is unhealthy, these are the types of friendships that you feel drained by. You lack trust in or peace about them. A toxic friend might gossip about you behind your back or belittle you or make you look bad around others to make themselves feel better. (Or you may find yourself doing this to friends when you're the one in a state of unhealth.)

A couple years ago, I had to part ways with a dear friend due to toxicity. After years of friendship, I began noticing that she'd try to keep me for herself, she'd gossip about me to others, she didn't encourage me in my faith, and she was never happy for me when something good happened. Losing her was unbelievably painful. Sometimes the death of a friendship hurts more than the death of a romantic relationship. But part of growing up is growing apart from people—and learning to be okay with it. It requires a certain amount of self-awareness and maturity to see unhealthy patterns and know when to pull the plug on a relationship. Some friendships may just need a step back for a season, but others may need to be entirely laid down. Only you can fully assess that, but I encourage you to seek reconciliation and a conversation before doing either one.

Healthy friendships require healthy communication and healthy conflict. If you're feeling hurt by someone and sliding toward resentment, then it's time to go to the person and tell them, not someone else. Sometimes people don't even know they are hurting us or have unhealthy habits because no one told them. The Bible is clear that God wants us to seek reconciliation whenever possible. However, reconciliation requires two people who desire it. Matthew 18:15–19 lays out a picture of how to deal with conflict in the church, and the initial steps can be applied to friendship as well. You first go to them and try to work it out; if they don't listen, bring a friend or two to help mediate. If they still don't listen, it might be acceptable to part ways. But you always go to them first and try to address the issue, not to others first to slander their name.

MY TOP NINE TIPS FOR HEALTHY
CONVERSATIONS WHEN CONFLICT ARISES

1. Pray before having a hard conversation.
2. Always take ownership for your part. "I know I talked bad about you to others before going to you first, and I'm sorry for that. Will you forgive me?"
3. Use "I" statements. For example, "I feel hurt when you make fun of me around our guy friends. It makes me feel like you want them to not like me." Not, "You are so rude and always put me down! You are such an insecure and horrible friend."
4. Don't use superlatives like "always" or "never"!
5. Speak slowly and gently. Don't use a sarcastic or bitter tone.
6. Give them time to respond, and listen to them. Rephrase their response and repeat it back to them to make sure you understood.
7. Be honest *and* loving.
8. Believe the best in them.
9. Forgive them, but potentially limit their access to you going forward.

In the end, we must remember that we cannot change people. We cannot control what they say or do; we can only control how we respond and react to them. So if they don't handle the conversation well, you can still know you tried and did your part. Sometimes the healthiest thing we can do in these scenarios is just let go of it for some time, pray that God would mend it eventually, pray for them, forgive them, refuse to talk bad about them, and continue on with our lives. Some people are part of our lives forever, and others just for a season. Thank them for what they taught you, and then keep living your life!

I pray this chapter helped you see a bit more how God desires friendships to be and not be! I know for many people, loneliness is more comfortable and feels easier than being vulnerable and facing potential rejection. But it's better to try and then fail than never try at all. What if it all goes right in the end? It requires taking a leap of faith to know! Let's be people who seek out good friends, and also be the friend people are looking for.

MAKE IT REAL IN YOUR LIFE

1. Where do you need to challenge yourself more in being a better friend?
2. What quality of being a good friend do you need to work on the most?
3. What new thing can you try in an attempt to find more friends?
4. Who do you need to reach out to check up on and care for?

5

Dating

How to Date in a Godly Way

O h, dating . . . the big daunting topic. I think everyone loves talking about dating because we all love the *idea of love*. It's been instilled in us ever since we were kids watching Disney movies, where the prince sweeps the princess off her feet. Questions surrounding dating are also probably the most common DMs that I receive. And I get why! It's tough out there, y'all. Dating is so complicated and dynamic because there is not a one-size-fits-all approach. It has so much nuance to it, there's no formal rule book, and the Bible doesn't talk much about dating, unfortunately, since our modern idea of it has only been around for about a hundred years.

In my own dating history, whether self-induced or others-inflicted, I've seen some things. From awkward first dates, failed talking stages, ghosting, cheating, and painful breakups to codependency, toxic relationships, and just not dating with wisdom, I've encountered it all.

Unfortunately, I'm not the only one. Based on my friends' experiences and my own—not to mention what I see on social media or reality TV—dating in our culture seems to be getting more confusing and complicated. I'm no dating expert, but I have learned so much through many people and resources and have made great strides to be healthy in this area.

Even though the Bible doesn't talk much about dating, it does talk about marriage and gives certain qualities of what to look for in a spouse, how to treat people, how to be wise, and how to be godly within the relationship. There are wrong and right ways to date. I've seen dating and relationships drastically, negatively affect people (like me), but I've also seen good, healthy, godly relationships cause people to flourish in so many ways. The Bible has some great principles that can be applied to both the negatives and positives of dating. So thankfully, there is hope!

Throughout this chapter, I'm going to give all my best tips that I've learned and seen work within dating. We have a lot to cover. Dating could be an entire book, but we'll stick to a chapter for now, so let's go!

What To Look For in a Partner

In your dating journey, you'll want to know what you're looking for in a potential partner.

Dating whoever crosses your path or strikes your fancy, without some parameters, can be more confusing and cause you to potentially date the wrong person because you don't have a guideline of what you're looking for. It's like grocery shopping without a shopping list while you're hungry; you'll impulse-buy anything without sound reason. Now, I'm not saying be too rigid with this list, especially when it comes to physicality, but do have a list of characteristics, nonnegotiables, values, and qualities that are important to you and your future. These qualities are something we should look for and consider both in others and in ourselves.

Not only will this list help you clearly know what you are looking for so you can avoid the wrong person, but it may also increase your self-worth and value, because not just *anyone* can date you! The person you marry has the potential to bring you a lot of joy or a lot of pain, so let's choose carefully.

Here are some qualities to look for in a partner.

A committed follower of Christ

As a Christian, you will want to date someone of the same faith as you, someone who is walking daily with Christ. This will help your overall relationship go a lot smoother, since you will both have the common goal to know Jesus and make him known. The way you date and pursue each other will drastically change as well if you date with the intention to honor God and honor each other. I advise you to avoid dating someone who doesn't share your faith or who isn't actively living out their faith. The Bible tells us in 2 Corinthians 6:14 not to be unequally yoked with an unbeliever, which means do not attach yourself to someone who isn't going in the same direction. I made this criteria number one because it will lay a foundation for the rest of the list.

Regarding a new believer, it's typically best to avoid dating some-one who is a new Christian, as they are still quite new to the faith and will have a lot to learn and grow in. You don't have to write them off forever; just give them time to grow on their own in the Lord. You'll want them to have worked through some of their struggles and questions before dating you.

This decision will affect the rest of your life: how they love you, your weekly routines, how you raise children, where you go to church, how you spend money, how you handle conflict, and so much more. Additionally, someone with different priorities or values can even-tually cause your own faith to decline, potentially leading you into some sin you wouldn't have entertained on your own. It's not worth ignoring just because you like someone. The more you spend time with someone, the more you become like them, so pick someone you'd be proud to become more like.

A friend of mine compromised on this and massively regrets it. Their marriage is constantly tough because her husband's goal is not to love her like Jesus would call him to but is instead based on however he feels that day. He doesn't lead her closer to the Lord, doesn't like to pray with her when things get tough, has a temper, and doesn't value spending his time and money to help others know Jesus. Compromising on this can lead to potential disaster down the road. Make sure *before* marrying someone that you know for sure they are committed to knowing God and honoring him with their life.

Respectful

Respect can make or break a relationship. You will want to be with someone who respects you and who you respect as well. Respect can look like them honoring your boundaries, your pace, your values, your job, your family, and just overall who you are—even when it inconveniences them or isn't something they understand. Respect should be a basic foundational pillar in your relationship.

If someone cannot respect your boundaries or you in general, that isn't your person. If someone keeps pushing you to do things you don't want to do or that are beyond your comfort zone, imagine what other boundaries they don't respect in many other areas of their life. You won't want to tie yourself to someone you constantly have to beg to honor you. You should never have to beg for the bare minimum.

On the flip side, if you don't respect the person you're with, it will be hard to want to listen to them, take their advice, maintain genuine affection, and trust their leadership. The Bible shows us how love and respect are key between a wife and a husband, as we can see in Ephesians 5:33 (ESV): "However, let each one of you love his wife as himself, and let the wife see that she respects her husband." Find a person worthy of respect, and continue to give it time to see if they consistently pursue you with respect.

In healthy community

This one might sound a bit weird, but it's really important! If they hang out with people who are negative or who encourage unhealthy behavior, that can eventually bleed into their relationship with you. You'll want to be with someone who has godly friends who encourage them in their faith, walk in accountability with them, and refine them—just like you want for yourself! Their friends will shape who they are.

Furthermore, you will want to see how they maintain and handle friendships. If someone is constantly jumping from friend group to friend group and doesn't have any long-lasting, authentic friendships where they are fully known, that might be a yellow flag. It shows they lack the commitment to maintain long-term friendships and might be running from friendships when things get hard instead of working through conflict. This is something they can work on, but you should proceed with caution.

Keep in mind that if you marry this person, their friends will be a part of your life too—and these people may be who you will need to depend on when things get tough. Hopefully they are caring, praying friends who will be there to support you both when you need it. Again, even if they have only a few close friends, that's better than none. Their community matters!

The fruit of the Spirit

I could ask you about a ton of qualities, but I think a great question to sum it all up would be this: *Do they display the fruit of the Spirit in their own life and with you?* Maybe this phrase is new for you, and you aren't sure what "the fruit of the Spirit" means, but we can find how God defines it in Galatians 5:22–23 (ESV, emphasis added): "But the fruit of the Spirit is *love, joy, peace, patience, kindness, goodness, faithfulness, gentleness, self-control.*" In John 15:8, it tells us that people will know we are Christ followers by these fruits. The fruit of the Spirit are qualities that God's people should possess by walking with him.

This also plays into dating. All these qualities are something that we should strive to have and look for in a person. Read the list again, and ponder how those will all be extremely beneficial in a partner. When sexual temptations come in the dating phase, can they be self-controlled and patient to wait for marriage? When something doesn't go their way, can they still be gentle and kind? When they are frustrated with you, can they still be loving toward you? When you maybe gain a little weight or aren't feeling your best, can they remain faithful to you? Kindness and goodness will also be evident in how they treat restaurant servers, store clerks, and strangers.

Keep in mind that no one can do these perfectly, but you want to be with someone who values these qualities and displays them as they continue to draw closer to God. These are byproducts of spending time with God, being around other believers, and living a life that wants to honor God.

Integrity

Integrity influences so many facets of someone's life, such as how they work, how they speak, and what they do when no one is watching. Integrity is living in the light. Someone with integrity doesn't lie to you, doesn't cheat on you, doesn't steal from their job, works hard even when their boss isn't looking, and consumes media that honors God. It would be very scary to date or marry someone who acts a certain way only when you're around.

Living a life of honesty and integrity is doing what's right even when no one is looking (see 2 Corinthians 8:21). When someone walks in integrity, it allows you to trust them more. Be with someone who is the same with both open and closed doors. Who they are with doors closed will eventually manifest somewhere in the open, so pay attention and give it time to see the signs. Don't ignore red flags. And make sure that you are a person of integrity as you pursue relationships.

TWELVE TOP QUALITIES TO PURSUE IN A PARTNER

Considering there are many other amazing qualities to look for in a person that I cannot go fully into, I want to create a high-level list of things I would advise you to think about and look for in a partner.

1. Are they teachable? Can they take correction and feedback? (Proverbs 15:32)
2. Are they a diligent, hard worker? (Proverbs 12:14)
3. Are they selfless and willing to go out of their way for you? (Ephesians 5:25)
4. Do they honor God with their time, actions, words, and thoughts? (1 Corinthians 10:31)
5. Do they communicate and handle conflict well? (Matthew 18:15–22, James 1:19)
6. Do they serve you and others in the community? (Romans 12:10; Hebrews 10:24)
7. Do they judge you and your past? (2 Corinthians 5:17)
8. Do they have any addictions they haven't dealt with? (Galatians 5:16)
9. What is their reputation? (1 Peter 2:12; Proverbs 22:1)
10. Do they respect authority? (Hebrews 13:17)
11. Do you enjoy being around them? Is it easy and fun to be with them even in the mundane? (Proverbs 17:22)
12. Do you feel free to be fully yourself with them? (2 Corinthians 3:17; Galatians 5:13)

Dating Mistakes to Avoid

In the dating phase, there's unfortunately a lot of room for error. I had to learn the hard way that making someone your entire world goes south pretty fast once they break up with you. I dated someone for nine months when I lived in California, and I really thought we would be married. Why? Because he told me so. Because of that, I let my guard down and I did everything and anything for this man. I would drive hours to see him every weekend, cook for him, buy him things, take care of him, and ditch my friends for him. I thought he needed me! Boy, was I wrong. When he broke up with me, I was absolutely devastated. Like the couldn't-eat-or-get-out-of-bed type of devastation. It was an overly emotional relationship with no boundaries. Looking back now, I can 100 percent see that it was not a good relationship; he and I are better off not together. Since then, I've learned a lot more about what to do and not do. Here are some things to avoid:

Rushing things

My number-one advice is to avoid rushing into things. This can look like talking about marriage early on, saying, "I love you" too quickly, getting physical, posting excessively about each other on social media, or talking about your future children. There is wisdom and discernment in taking things slowly. Even though you may think you know the person from day one, you don't. True colors, whether good or bad, will always be revealed over time.

Make time your best friend. Within three to six months or even later, you'll start to see who people really are. It never hurts to take things slowly, get to know the person, bring them around your friends, ask them good questions, and see if you even enjoy who they are and being with them before letting feelings override wisdom. Usually people *don't* say, "Man, I wish we went faster!" They usually say, "We wish we took things slower."

You really want to see who this person is in multiple situations and circumstances to evaluate their character. Anyone can be exactly what you want for the short-term, but over time, any facade or fabrication eventually fades. I once dated a guy I really liked, and who I thought liked me too since he kept telling me I was "wifey material." Two months in, I found out he was dating another girl at the same time! Boy, bye! I'm thankful I didn't give this man my heart or make him my boyfriend, because after only two months, his true colors were revealed.

I wouldn't recommend becoming officially boyfriend-girlfriend with someone until you have been exclusively going on dates with them for at least two to three months. Infatuation in the beginning stages can get you to do and say some strange things and overlook red flags, so enjoy the journey and each step along the way without rushing to the next one.

Even though I know many people who have gotten engaged after six months, those people had spent an unusually large amount of time with their partner, brought them around their friends and family, didn't cross physical boundaries, and honored God in the process. I wouldn't always recommend this method for everyone, but if you date well and feel that God and others bless it, it could work. Remember, though, "Every idea seems like a good idea in isolation."[1] So don't date in isolation. Always involve God and his people in the process for protection and more wisdom. It will definitely benefit you.

Lacking boundaries

Boundaries are important in dating, because having good ones helps set a healthy tone, pace, and safeguard for protection around your heart before marriage. Song of Solomon 8:4 says, "Daughters of Jerusalem, I charge you: Do not arouse or awaken love until it so desires." Meaning, do not awaken your heart to love or sexuality until its proper time. Solomon instructs this because before marriage, awakening love and passion for this person will cause you to mesh together before making a real covenant, causing you to feel like you've become one when you actually have not. It's very hard to undo once it's already done.

What happens if the person leaves or you break up? When there are no boundaries, it may feel like a divorce without an actual marriage. Boundaries say, "We are not married; therefore, we won't act like we are." It will not only protect you, your heart, and the relationship, but the other person too. It's treating the relationship as a deeper friendship until you have a real commitment and covenant in marriage.

Lack of physical boundaries can mean kissing too soon, sleeping in the same bed, moving in together, doing everything but sex, and having sex before marriage. Call me old-fashioned, but I think God's design for marriage and sexuality is a purposeful and beautiful thing. I didn't do these perfectly before marriage, but I sure wish I did. I'll share more of my story later in the book, but for now, I'll say I've seen the negative side of not following these boundaries well.

These lines blur very quickly and can make you feel overly attached to someone. Sex releases chemicals such as dopamine, oxytocin, and vasopressin in the brain,[2] which all create powerful emotional bonds. They bond you to someone or something, such as porn, and may cause you to feel addicted or in love, when in reality you are just forming a chemical bond.

I am not trying to take away your fun or shame you if you have been or are sexually active, but rather show you that sex is God's design made for marriage. It's for God's protection over you that he designed it this way. Sex outside of marriage can result in shame, fear of pregnancy, fear of STDs, lack of real trust with the person, feeling used, and lower rational thinking about the relationship. Your sexual desires are not wrong or bad, because God created them, but they're meant to be for one person in the sacred context of marriage. Trust that God designed this plan out of his love for you! Even if you've already crossed the line, it's never too late to start over again. God still loves you and sees you as worthy!

Rushing into physicality and engaging in intercourse disrupts your journey of truly getting to know someone. Instead of having good conversations, spending time doing other activities, and using self-control, you'll opt to be intimate. It's low-hanging fruit that's easy to run to when you're bored, or if it's awkward between you two, or if you both are feeling impatient. If your relationship ends, it may cause the breakup to feel even more painful once these bonds have been formed.

Finding someone who is also committed to sexual integrity will help you both commit to having sex only in marriage with your spouse. Set this boundary very early on in your relationship, tell people about it, and know what will trigger you to fall into temptation. Waiting to have sex until marriage may be tough, but asking God and others for help will make it easier. Ultimately, practicing sexual integrity is worth it, and it continues within marriage.

Spiritual boundaries are important for maintaining your own intimacy with God and not depending on someone for your faith. Regardless of whether you are dating or married, you will always need to have your own relationship with Jesus. Lacking spiritual boundaries can look like reading your Bible only when you're with your partner, praying only with them (never on your own), only going to church when they go, and generally merging your relationship with Christ with theirs. It can be dangerous when you don't really know who God is for yourself, and you depend on this person for your faith.

If you are not married to them, you may think that this person is your spiritual leader, when that's the role God gave a husband, not a boyfriend (Ephesians 5:25–30). Of course, you can go to church together, you can worship together, and you can pray for one another, but have boundaries. Don't make this person your god, your pathway to God, or an idol in your life. Don't let your relationship with your partner replace your personal relationship with God.

Good boundaries are ultimately about maintaining healthy independence. I know this may seem a bit legalistic, but boundaries will guard your heart in the relationship until marriage. Playing house or marriage typically doesn't go well if the relationship ends— and while you may believe your relationship will never end, only a marriage covenant truly protects that. Once you are married, the boundaries completely shift and change. But relationships don't have to hurt so badly or end so painfully if you date well with good boundaries.

OTHER BOUNDARIES TO CONSIDER

Boundaries draw the line between dating and marriage. They say, "Before marriage, we will not ____" (fill in the blank). Here are some of my recommendations of things to avoid:

1. Living together before marriage
2. Engaging in any kind of sexual acts before marriage
3. Dating in isolation, where no one knows what or how you are doing
4. Confiding and confessing *only* to one another about struggles
5. Talking *only* to each other about your faith
6. Spending every waking moment together
7. Dropping everyone and everything for each other
8. Saying "I love you" too quickly, until you know the true meaning and can show it consistently in your actions

---

Dating Well

Dating will result in either a breakup or marriage. I know this may feel a bit daunting, but it's true! If you don't want to waste your time or someone else's, date with the intention of it leading toward marriage and honoring them in the process. Even if a relationship doesn't work out, if you've dated well, you can end on good terms and with nothing but respect for one another. Dating doesn't always have to be a disaster! Here are some of my tips for dating well.

Clarity

As you are dating, you and the other person should be clear with each other about your intentions and where you are with the relationship. If you are not feeling like moving forward in the relationship, be up-front and honest yet kind: "Hey, I really am grateful for you pursuing me the way you have, but I just don't see this moving forward." Clarity is honoring to the other person by being thoughtful of their emotions and desires for the relationship.

Honesty

Sometimes, because we are afraid of hurting the other person, we lie to make them happy. In the long run, this is actually more damaging because the person will believe your words and may eventually find out you didn't actually mean them, which may be very hurtful. Saying you like something that they like (but you really don't) in order to make them like you more is a facade. It creates a false foundation for the relationship. Saying things you don't actually mean—like "I want to marry you" or "I love you"—out of trying to avoid ruffling some feathers is just dishonest and breaks trust. A healthy relationship requires communication, honesty, trust, and healthy conflict. Do not say things out of impulse or emotion just to make someone feel good in the moment. It's okay to take time to respond and process how you feel. They won't feel good later if they see your words were a lie. Be a person of your word! Your honesty doesn't have to be hurtful, just truthful. Pray for discernment on how and when to say it.

Quit playing games

I think one of the most hurtful things in dating is when one person is taking it seriously while the other person is not. We all know dating has gotten extremely confusing and frustrating in the last decade, thanks to social media, dating apps, and our increasingly complicated culture, but it doesn't have to stay this way—we can change the narrative. Some people seem to actually love playing mind games. They love to feel affection and attention (even from someone they may not actually like) to enhance their self-esteem at the expense of someone else. Sometimes we may not mean to, but out of fear or a past wound, we hurt people in the process, possibly perpetuating these poor dating habits further. It's why healing your past wounds so you don't bleed on other people is so important.

To avoid playing games, go back to the first two points. If you're not seriously interested in someone or don't want to go on another date with them, kindly tell them. Do not ghost them or play basketball with their heart by going back and forth with how you feel. People's hearts are not something for you to uncaringly dispose of whenever you feel like it. You wouldn't want someone to do this to you either. I know many situations aren't black and white, but pray for God's clarity in the process to avoid hurting someone further.

Recognize the right relationship

If you think you've found a good person, pray that God would show you quickly if this is someone you should marry. Look at the qualities on the list I mentioned earlier, and see if this person has some of them. Bring them around your friends and in multiple different situations to see how they react and respond. Have your friends and family ask you challenging questions about the relationship. Watch their actions over a long period of time to see who they really are. Keep your heart and boundaries guarded so you don't cloud your judgment when trying to make a decision, and know that your feelings about this person are real but not always reliable. You may feel in love, but use biblical wisdom, not just how you feel, to decide if this is the right person for the long haul. Finally, enjoy the ride! Dating should be fun, easy, and low pressure! You don't need to know if you are marrying someone on the first or third date. If you are severely lacking peace about this person, we'll talk about that next.

When and How to Break Up

The part of relationships that are never fun. I pray no one has to go through a breakup, but if you do or already have, then this one's for you. Breakups can be painful, especially if you thought the person was your forever. I've been through my fair share of breakups, whether I was the one breaking up with someone or being broken up with, so I know the feeling! Here are my tips on when to break up.

If you are in a relationship and considering calling it quits with your boo thang, here are my thoughts. Typically, if you're in a relationship and already feeling like you want to end it, then you should strongly pray through this. That may be your spirit telling you it's wrong. I would first process with trusted friends about the relationship and see what they think, because they can help you discern if you are just trying to run away out of fear or if this genuinely isn't the best, godly relationship for you. But if you are feeling a major lack of peace with this person, or like they don't truly make you a better person, or there is major sin, or they have red flags, or overall you just cannot see this being a good fit for your future and future children, then you may not want to tie yourself up with this person. If you find that others also don't think this is a healthy, good relationship for you, it's definitely worth listening to. I remember I had a relationship where I ignored godly counsel, and I severely regretted it. Marriage isn't a light thing to commit to flippantly. Red flags and problems won't magically go away in marriage, they actually amplify. So whatever problems you are having now, think about that amplifying and being in a covenant with it. Choose wisely.

A girl recently sent me a DM saying she was contemplating ending her relationship, but she didn't want to only because she was afraid of being twenty-eight and single again. Continuing a relationship out to fear of being alone is absolutely not a good reason to stay. Marrying the wrong person because you're afraid of being alone will lead you to be married and still feel alone. It's better to end the relationship now, not when the time is "right," so you can heal, move on, and eventually find the right person God has for you.

I know this may feel absolutely terrifying, especially if you love the person or have been with them for a while, but it is better to be single than settle. Breaking up with the person should come with a lot of prayer and counsel first, but your future self will thank you. When ending it with this person, end with clarity, kindness, honesty, and affirmation, and clearly cut ties.

This can look like the following: "I'm ending our relationship because I don't feel peace about this. I do not think we are a good fit for each other in marriage. I'm very sad about this and I care about you so much, but I spent time with the Lord and feel this is the best. I think it's best if we do not communicate again after this, unless you really need something. Thank you for all you've done for me and taught me. I truly appreciate you, and I wish you nothing but the best in your future."

Add whatever you need and make it personal to you, but this is an example of a breakup I've actually been through that went really well, despite it still being painful. Remember, be kind and loving by being honest.

Healing from a Breakup

Maybe you've initiated a breakup, or maybe you've been the person someone broke up with and you're really going through it. I wish I could give you a big hug and tell you that it's going to be okay. I know breakups not only hurt our hearts but also come with fears, such as fearing you'll never find someone again, or that you're unlovable, or that you lost "your person" permanently. These are all very valid feelings, but stick with me. I would never wish a breakup on anyone, but if you're here, now what?

First, breakups take time. They just do. Let yourself cry, talk about it, and grieve. You can't rush healing. Unfortunately, you have to go through it fully. Try not to suppress the feelings; instead, journal and pray through them. Some find it helpful to go by the six-month rule, which says that it takes around six months of healing time for every year we are with someone. In other words, it will take time depending on the length of your relationship. Even short relationships need plenty of time to heal! Take it from me.

Use this time to get as healthy as possible. Process with friends regularly. Discuss the relationship with a counselor if you need to. Go on trips with your friends. Work out and reach a goal, or start a new hobby. Go on walks and listen to some podcasts or audiobooks on godly relationships. Learn a new recipe. Give yourself this time to grow and learn more about yourself. Pray to God and ask him to heal your heart. In Psalm 34:18, he says he's near to you when your heart is broken. He cares for you deeply. Lean on God during this time. It's okay to cry and still feel sadness even after some time has passed. But trust that God is with you in the pain.

The less exposure you have to your ex, the quicker you'll heal. Cut off as much communication with and reminders of them as you can. This can mean unfollowing, blocking, or muting them on social media. Avoid looking at old photos and listening to old songs that remind you of them. I know this can be very difficult, but a pause will help a lot. After I went through a breakup one time, I wasn't ready to delete all the pictures yet, so I hid them until I was fully ready to remove them all. It took me six months to finally delete the pictures, but it sure was helpful not seeing them all over my camera roll.

See where you need to grow personally. Often, we want to shift blame and point all the fingers at the other person, never reflecting on where we still need some growth. Even though one person in the relationship may have done more damage than the other, it's always important to ask yourself, "Where were my faults?" instead of only seeing theirs (Matthew 7:5). In your time of growth, work on forgiving the person if they hurt you (Ephesians 4:32). I know this can be extremely challenging to do, but forgiveness means you don't leave room for bitterness in your heart and let the enemy work in that. Forgiveness will also set you up for healthiness in your next relationship when you no longer have resentment toward your ex.

When you feel yourself missing them or wanting to get back together with them, write down all the areas in the relationship that weren't good or healthy and reflect on those. We tend to remember only the good moments and get tunnel vision when there may have been a plethora of bad qualities that ultimately caused the relationship to end. Reflect on why the relationship ended and what you were missing in it. Do not run back out of loneliness, insecurities, or boredom. It's okay to miss them, but just because you miss them doesn't mean that you're meant to be with them.

Avoid running to someone else or something to numb the pain. Numbing is only delaying healing. I know breakups can make you feel lonely to the point that you just need something to help you cope, but another person or thing—like alcohol or shopping—won't heal your heart like time and Jesus will. It's healthy to have some time alone to heal and be with the Lord before jumping into another situation. Don't let your fears or feelings dictate God's plan for you. Have friends help you do this too!

Trust God in the process, which I know may be the hardest thing to do. Surrender the relationship to God, and ask him to show you why he protected you from this relationship going any further. We don't know why God does things sometimes, but we can trust his character and believe that his plans are to prosper us, not to harm us (Jeremiah 29:11). God won't take something away for no reason or purpose. Taking it away may have been the biggest blessing for you down the road.

Finally, if you are in an abusive relationship, please seek help! If someone is verbally, emotionally, or physically abusing you, tell someone you know and trust, or call the National Domestic Violence Hotline at 800-799-7233 (or text "Start" to 88788). God's intention was never for you to be used and abused. You are so valuable to him!

As I close out this chapter, I'm praying for the person who feels lonely, hopeless, or alone. Your story is not done being written. Your heavenly Father loves you too much to leave you feeling disappointed or distraught. Know that your relationship with Jesus matters the most above all others. Your relationship with God will influence every other relationship. Prioritize him and make him your first love. You will never regret it.

I hope all these tips can help you on this journey of dating. And if you are already engaged or married, maybe they can be reminders of what a godly relationship looks like, or some things to reengage into your current relationship. Relationships can go a lot smoother if we all do our part to love one another, seek the goodness of others, and honor one another. Let's date well, friends!

MAKE IT REAL IN YOUR LIFE

1. What boundaries do you need to set for yourself and your relationships?
2. What dating mistakes have you made in the past?
3. How have you handled a breakup poorly in the past?
4. What ways can you honor someone better going forward?
5. What was the most important lesson you learned from this chapter?

6

Confidence

Overcoming Insecurities and Becoming Secure

At ten years old, you could have found me in the bathroom looking in the mirror being pretty ticked off with God. Why, you ask? I was pretty upset with him for how he made me look. Growing up in a predominantly white neighborhood, church, and school, I didn't understand why God didn't make me look like my peers. He gave me brown hair, brown eyes, and tan skin from my Guatemalan heritage, but I thought that being beautiful meant being tall, skinny, blond, and blue-eyed. I was so disappointed in God for how he made me, I would literally cry to myself in the mirror.

My sisters and I were often teased in school for being "mutts" (i.e., being mixed-race). I'm half German and half Guatemalan. This isn't to say "Woe is me . . . my life is so hard," but to simply share with you, I get what it's like being insecure, lacking confidence, and disliking yourself. I wish I could say I overcame those insecurities shortly after, but that would be a lie. It took me a whopping fifteen years. I was around twenty-five before I finally felt more confident and secure in who God created me to be. All those fifteen years consisted of me doing anything and everything to fit in and be liked.

Buying more Abercrombie shirts (that I couldn't afford), dyeing my hair, wearing colored contacts, wearing knockoff designer clothes, and begging my dad to help me get the latest iPhone or Razr phone (yes, I'm that old!) so I could fit in.

When I went to college, it only got worse. Out of this painful place of such disdain for myself, my insecurities made me like a chameleon. I camouflaged into whomever and whatever someone wanted me to be in order to be liked, because that's all I wanted to be. Yet even though I did all the camouflaging and morphing, I was still unhappy. College Jeanine didn't grasp that confidence and security didn't come from external adornments but rather from an internal knowing of how much God loved her, regardless of her appearance.

I can imagine God looking down on me feeling sad—sadness for his daughter, whom he designed exactly how he meant her to be, yet here she was, trying to change every single facet. It's like I took an eraser to the art piece he drew and said, "This is ugly, and you messed up. Let me fix it!" Imagine how the artist would feel. Pretty discouraged, huh? That's what the majority of us do every single day. As we get dressed, do our makeup, brush our hair, and look in the mirror, we nitpick all the little things we wish we could change about ourselves. All while God sits on his throne, smiling at the very thought of who you are, because he fearfully and wonderfully made you (Psalm 139:14) with intentionality and purpose. He didn't make a mistake. He never does. You are his masterpiece and handiwork (Ephesians 2:10)!

This chapter is harder to write because I don't think it's something we will ever fully overcome, but something we must continually strive to be conscientious of. In a world of perfect-looking people scrolling past our eyes at an exponential rate, it's no wonder we nitpick ourselves and wish we looked different. I remember seeing someone on TikTok post their nose job surgery, and I suddenly began to think, *Hmm . . . I kind of want a nose job now.* And I fixated on it for a while. I went down a rabbit hole of videos of girls who got their noses redone, and I began to feel jealous that they had a cute button nose and I didn't. I let culture, society, and social media dictate whether I thought I was beautiful, instead of God. Maybe you feel this way too. Maybe you're experiencing this right now.

I understand that appearance plays a massive role in one's confidence, and I don't want to be cheesy and slap a Bible verse on you and say, "Just read Psalm 139:14 again and all your insecurities will go away!" but to instead challenge you to truly meditate on it, and often. Let it transform you from the inside out. What we consume is what we become. What we input is what we output. If we are trying to determine what beauty looks like only by the world's standards, none of us will ever be enough, because the world's standards are ever changing, while God's Word is unchanging. If we let social media consumption dictate how we deem ourselves, why can't we let God's Word even more ultimately define our true value? Our worth and value cannot only come from social media comments or affirmations from men and our peers, because that will be fleeting and unstable. It should come from the Word of God and his words being written on our hearts.

Who does God say we are? I could go on and on about who he says we are, but here are a few of my favorite verses:

1. *God's workmanship*—"For we are his workmanship, created in Christ Jesus for good works, which God prepared beforehand, that we should walk in them" (Ephesians 2:10 ESV).
2. *Beautiful*—"You are altogether beautiful, my love; there is no flaw in you" (Song of Solomon 4:7 ESV).
3. *Wonderfully made*—"I praise you because I am fearfully and wonderfully made; your works are wonderful, I know that full well" (Psalm 139:14).
4. *Made in his image*—"So God created man in his own image, in the image of God he created him; male and female he created them" (Genesis 1:27 ESV).

These are truths we must cling to when the enemy tries to tell us otherwise. When we try to tell ourselves otherwise. Sometimes we are our own worst enemy.

The world would like to tell us that confidence comes from being a girl boss, having a ton of followers, a hot boyfriend, a slim-thick body, perfect glassy skin, or the dreamy high-rise apartment. But what if you got all of those and you still aren't happy or don't like yourself? Where does your confidence come from then? We can only fake it for so long. Fake it till you make it goes only so far.

First Peter 3:3–4 says, "Your beauty should not come from outward adornment, such as elaborate hairstyles and the wearing of gold jewelry or fine clothes. Rather, it should be that of your inner self, the unfading beauty of a gentle and quiet spirit, which is of great worth in God's sight." Confidence has to be something that ultimately comes from within and from God. Remembering and understanding the true meaning of the verse above will change the way you see yourself.

Confidence comes with time, self-work, prayer, healing, positive self-talk, counseling, talking with friends, and maturity—it did for me, at least. I am not encouraging you to stop shopping, putting on makeup, doing your hair, or doing anything that helps boost your confidence. I, for one, love rocking a new outfit, getting my nails done, and feeling good about how I look. But these should never override how you feel on the inside about yourself. External additions cannot cancel out internal insecurities; we must address the internal insecurities first. The additions should come from an overflow of acceptance and gladness for who you already are—as a form of expression.

Using external things as a mask when you don't truly like or accept yourself will eventually become a facade. They will slowly but surely fade away and the truth will manifest itself somehow. I know that is harsh to say, but I've seen this truth play out in my own life. I did the classic tear-another-girl-down-because-I-don't-like-myself move a ton. Even if I felt good about myself one day, if a guy affirmed my friend but not me, I instantly became jealous and threw a quick jab at her in an attempt to make myself seem better. That is pretty insecure and petty of me, don't ya think? It screams, *Pick me!*

I know overcoming insecurities will not happen overnight, but I believe it's possible. It's how you talk to yourself daily, what you let yourself believe about yourself, what you consume, and how you replace the lies with truth. When you are beating yourself up with negative self-talk and picking yourself apart, I encourage you to think about the following:

What would you tell a friend? Would you tell her that she looks fat, ugly, or has an ugly feature about herself? Or would you encourage her?

What would you tell your daughter? Would you talk to your potential future daughter the way you talk to yourself? If you have a daughter now, could you imagine speaking to her the way you speak to yourself?

What would you tell your younger self? What does your younger self need to hear? Would she be proud to know that her future self belittles herself?

What you think is what you become (Proverbs 23:7 NKJV); be intentional with how you think about yourself.

What Is More Important?

Your appearance should be the least interesting thing about you. Hot take, I know! But imagine if you walked out of a room full of people and everyone only said, "Dang . . . she is so hot. She has the best body!" To me, "Wow, she is the kindest person and really radiates God's joy," is much more a compliment than commenting on my outside beauty. I don't think there is anything wrong with beauty or wanting to feel pretty, but to make that your ultimate goal in life is fleeting and vain. Proverbs 31:30 says, "Charm is deceptive, and beauty is fleeting; but a woman who fears [has reverence for] the LORD is to be praised." I would much rather be a woman known for how I love God and love people than for how pretty or hot I was. Looks fade; character remains. Let your character be the most attractive thing about you.

I would feel really sad if people were attracted to my physical appearance but determined I was ugly after getting to know me. This is why I think 1 Peter 3:3–4 talks about the importance of your inner self. We can dress up, work out, wear lipstick, and curl our hair, but if our inner self is hurting or doesn't genuinely care about people, it will show. The verse implies that the woman of God is gentle and quiet not because she has to be, but because someone who is confident doesn't need to be the center of attention by being loud. She doesn't have to flaunt or prove anything. She is secure in who God made her to be and doesn't need people to affirm her. That's why there's a quote saying, "Confidence is quiet, insecurities are loud." I'm not telling you how to behave, but be mindful of why you might feel the need to act a certain way.

This can manifest in dating too. In dating, it's important to be careful how we attract people, and be mindful of what we are attracted to. Marrying someone just for looks or trying to lure someone in by your looks is fleeting and deceiving. If looks fade and character remains, we want our character to be our most important and attractive feature for years to come. Find someone who is not just super hot and has abs but who genuinely has amazing character.

We can see a great example of this in the Bible with the story of Ruth. Ruth was a God-fearing woman whose husband had died. Instead of going back to her part of the country, she decided to remain with her mother-in-law, Naomi. She tells Naomi she will remain faithful to her and follow her wherever she goes, so they go back to Naomi's hometown of Bethlehem. Since it's time for the barley harvest, Ruth decides to glean from a field. Although she doesn't know it, the field she chooses belongs to a wealthy man named Boaz, who happens to be Naomi's relative. When Boaz visits the field and hears of Ruth's loyalty to Naomi, he instructs his workers to allow her to glean and leave additional grain in her path. In the end of the story, Boaz excitingly takes Ruth to be his wife. He tells her in Ruth 2:11 (ESV), "All that you have done for your mother-in-law since the death of your husband has been fully told to me, and how you left your father and mother and your native land and came to a people that you did not know before."

Notice how Boaz never talks about her appearance (even though I'm sure he thought she was beautiful); he admires her character. This story shows her traits of faithfulness, commitment, hard work, faith in God, honor, and humility. Beauty is beneficial, but it cannot make up for a lack of character.

Where Do Insecurities Come From?

When I was in middle school, I was a bit flat-chested and was definitely part of the bra-stuffing club. I even didn't care that much about my chest size until some guy friends in seventh grade told me they thought I had small boobs. We were all on the phone one night, and they all chuckled and said, "Jeanine . . . you have small boobs!" My eyes welled up with tears, I turned bright red, and I hung up the phone quickly. I was mortified! They tried calling me back to apologize, but I turned my phone off and ran to the mirror to examine my chest. Yep . . . *Confirming that I do have small boobs!* I cried. From that day forward, for most of middle school and some of high school, I began stuffing my bra and wearing bras way bigger than I had the right to wear, all out of insecurity.

I share this awkward and funny story to show you that our insecurities stem from somewhere. I didn't care much that I had a smaller chest until someone pointed it out. Out of that insecurity, I began to do some strange things just to prove people wrong. Thank God I don't do that anymore, but we all know middle school is a tough time!

Identifying why you feel the way you do is so important. I acted out of trying to disprove my friend's opinions, and more recently from the comments on my Instagram. But maybe for you, you've been trying to disprove something a parent told you, or an ex, or a friend. Or maybe it was seeing someone on social media have something you didn't. Ask yourself where the insecurities come from, because we cannot heal what we don't reveal.

The issue is that we give people's opinions so much more power than God's opinions. People don't care nearly as much as you think they do. We all tend to focus much more on how *we* look and if others like *us* than on what others are doing. We give people who don't even care that much way more equity than they deserve. Let that free you up: people don't care as much as you think they do. We're the ones who care too much. Sadly, we are our own worst critics.

In closing, here are some practical things to remember in this journey of becoming more confident:

1. A lack of confidence is often rooted in a lack of identity. If you don't know your identity in Christ, you will look for fleeting things to determine it. You might look to money, appearance, a relationship status, college, or followers to find affirmation. These things will never satisfy and can only temporarily make us feel fulfilled.

2. Practice creating eye contact with people to increase your confidence. Eye contact is an important nonverbal social cue that projects confidence, self-esteem, and assertiveness. Licensed and professional therapist Tameka Wade Brewington states, "People with good eye contact are seen as confident and as active listeners."[1] She also recommends, "A good rule of thumb to gauge eye contact is to use it 50 percent of the time you are talking and 70 percent of the time when you are listening."[2] Try it out next time you are having a conversation, even if it might feel a bit awkward at first!

3. The more you meditate on the truths of God, the more you will believe them and walk them out. Speaking life over yourself consistently will one day turn into you knowing and believing it!

4. Wear and do what helps. What I mean by this is, if wearing a certain color, style, or dress makes you feel more confident, do that! If doing your hair a certain way makes you feel your best, do it! If working out and feeling strong helps you boost your mood that day, do it! While I am not a big proponent of believing these things will solve our problems, I do believe they can help. Always remember to make sure you take care of your heart and inner self first.

5. Let yourself feel off some days! This last and final point is so vital, because often we put so much pressure on ourselves to be perfect and perform 24/7. It would be unrealistic to expect ourselves to always feel flawless and full of high self-esteem. There are going to be days that no matter what you do or how hard you try, you won't feel it, and that is okay! These are the days to remind yourself that you are human and no one has it all together. You don't have to feel like a victor every day to believe you are. This is when you look at yourself in the mirror and say, "I am still enough because Jesus says I am." Move on with your day and don't give feelings too much power. You are beautiful, no matter what someone has told you or you've told yourself. I pray you believe that today.

MAKE IT REAL IN YOUR LIFE

1. Where did your insecurity come from?
2. What are some negative things you tell yourself every day? What truths do you need to tell yourself instead?
3. Who do you feel you need to prove wrong or prove your worth to?
4. What three loving things can you say to yourself right now? What Scripture do you need to cling to in this season to believe you are who God says you are?

———— 7 ————

Habits

A Guide to Improve Your Day and Life

People often ask me how I am so disciplined and consistent, which I truly appreciate, but I wasn't always. You could look at my sleep schedule, my eating habits, lack of reading, lack of being active, and think, *Yikes, she's a pretty sloppy person.* And I was! I did whatever I wanted, whenever I wanted to. Procrastination was my addiction, staying up late watching Netflix was my hobby, and sugar was my kryptonite. I lacked any real routine, sleep schedule, fitness regime, or accountability. I struggled to finish a book, hated journaling, and failed at reading my Bible every day. My life reflected that. I was a mess. I was anxious, lethargic, my skin constantly broke out, I was always tired, overweight, and couldn't get myself to focus while studying. I knew something had to change.

In college, I gained quite a bit of weight due to drinking too much on the weekends, so I set out to lose some weight and get healthier. I made this grand plan: work out five times a week, no more carbs, no more sugar, salads for lunch, and veggies and chicken for dinner. I was determined! I set out on my little journey with so much excitement, only to fail after just one week. *Shocking.* I beat myself up; I was so disappointed in myself.

Ugh, I suck. Am I just that undisciplined and unmotivated? I tried attempting the plan again, and again, and again, only to fail over and over. *Why can't I do this? I'm such a failure!* I always told myself. But I didn't know that success doesn't happen overnight, in one week, or even a month, but rather daily, over a long amount of time. I didn't know the power of small decisions that lead to big disciplines. Where you will be in a year will be a reflection of the choices you make now. Where you are now is a reflection of the choices you made a year ago. This is what changed my lifestyle.

By now, you've heard me say the word *habit* a hundred times, because I think it has the power to change your life and help you become happier and healthier. When I changed my habits, then I knew Jesus more, read more, slept better, mentally grew more, worked out consistently, changed my eating patterns, and just overall felt better and healthier. So how do we do it? Let's begin!

Why Dramatic Changes Don't Last

People may look at someone they admire who is successful or disciplined and wonder, *Do they just have something I don't? Were they always like this?* Typically, the answer is no. The people you admire usually understand the power of small, daily choices and how they have more of an impact than a massive overnight change that may not last. In the book *Atomic Habits* by James Clear, he talks about the power of the 1 percent.

He discusses how a 1 percent improvement every single day for a year will result in being "thirty-seven times better by the time you're done."[1] A 1 percent increase may look small, but in the long run, it pays off if it's done consistently over time. Often people think that to make a change in their life, it needs to be this drastic, life-altering switch up, when in reality, that's not typically sustainable.

At the beginning of the year, people create all sorts of goals and make big statements for their New Year's resolutions but typically fail to stick to them. Unfortunately, we aren't very good at sticking to our grand goals. Maybe it's because we bite off more than we can chew. I've done this many times. I've said since 2016, "I want to write a book!" But I made no plan to get there. The Bible states in Proverbs 29:18 (KJV), "Where there is no vision, the people perish." My goal perished until I finally made a plan and executed it. This book is proof of me putting my plan into action.

How to Create Habits

It's important to first determine who you want to become or who you want to be.[2] Don't just say, "I want to run more"; get specific and declare, "I want to be someone who is a runner and runs at least three times a week." You live out who you think you are. What do you want to stand for? What are your principles and values? Who do you wish to become? Does this behavior help you become the person you want to be?

If I say I want to be someone who looks like Jesus, but my actions don't represent that, my desire is merely just words. State more specific goals, such as, "I want to be a Jesus follower who reads the Word daily, attends church weekly, serves at church once a month, gives away at least 10 percent of my income to someone in need, and meets weekly with other believers."

The reason so many goals fail is because they are too big or immeasurable. Once you define a goal and make a plan of action, it's easier to start the journey. This could look like researching more about your specific goal, narrowing down what it might take to get there, and trying to consistently do that action every day or week.

Your habits need to be realistic. Start small. The more specific and realistic you are with your goal, the easier it will be to obtain it. For example, if you want to start reading the Bible, instead of just saying, "I'm going to read my Bible" or even "I'm going to finish a book in the Bible this week," you can make a small plan of action like this: "For the next week, I'm going to read a verse a day." Start small and master that before taking on more work. Building habits takes time!

HAPPY, HEALTHY HABITS TO START TODAY

1. Drink a minimum of three glasses of water every day.
2. Take a ten-minute walk.
3. Make your bed every morning.
4. Read a chapter in the Bible daily.
5. Listen to a podcast while you clean once a week.
6. Call or text one friend every day.
7. Eat at least one vegetable per day.
8. Take a vitamin every morning.

Once you master a habit, then you can add more to it. You need to determine for yourself where your baseline is and what more you can add. For some, simply putting on workout clothes daily and going for a ten-minute walk is a win. For others, running two miles every day is already a habit they've mastered, and they are ready to add on another mile. Whatever your goal, start small, and realistically keep adding on to it.

START WITH THIS, NOT THAT

If you're just beginning to create habits like these, start small.

Try This	Not This
Walk ten minutes per day	Run a mile every day
Read a page in a book before bed	Read a chapter before bed
Eat a vegetable with your dinner every night	Eat vegetables and fruits every single meal

---

Make Your Habits Obvious and Easy

Something I've seen in my own life (and that James Clear talks about) is making your new habit so obvious that you can't resist it. The more you see something, the more likely you are to do it, which can be positive or negative. If you are trying to limit how much sugar you eat and you keep seeing candy in your home, you'll most likely want to eat it. Or if you are trying to drink more water, the more you see your water bottle, the more likely you are to drink water.

So, whatever you are trying to do (or not do), either add or remove it from your home and your sight. If you want to run more, put your running shoes out where you can see them. If you want to eat more fruits and veggies, buy them and make them visible on your counter and in your refrigerator. If you want to journal more, have it next to your bed so you'll see it before bedtime. We often will opt for what is easy and comfortable, including our past bad habits. Make the right choice easy and accessible.

A habit of mine is to lay out my workout clothing before I go to bed. That way when I wake up, I don't waste time picking out an outfit and having decision fatigue. I jump out of bed, put the outfit on, and don't think twice about it. The easier you can make it for yourself, the more likely you'll do it.

On the other hand, sometimes you need to remove things. I noticed that when I am trying to have my quiet times in the morning, my phone is a massive distraction. I will quite literally throw it across the room onto another couch so I get it away from me and out of my sight. If I don't do this, I will continue to reach for it and let it pull me away from my Bible. You know what they say: *Out of sight, out of mind*.

Make a Plan and Take Action

A plan without follow-through is just a plan. A successful plan requires action to it. If you were to go on a road trip, you wouldn't just

101

hop in the car and hope to end up at your destination. You would set yourself up for success! You would map it out, know where you're going to sleep overnight, buy snacks for the road, and have your music playlist ready to jam to. It's the same way when preparing to build a habit. If you want to prepare for ultimate success, you need to get the required items for the task and create a schedule or routine to do it.

For example, if you want to save money, you would:

1. Open a savings account with your bank.
2. Determine what you're saving for.
3. Set a daily or weekly savings goal. Remember, start small! Could just be $5 a day or per week.
4. Check your savings account to track your plan and note how rewarding it is to save money.
5. Once you get to your goal, treat yourself with something small as a reward and incentive to keep going. Psychologically this helps your brain to see this as something fun and rewarding to do, instead of sacrificial.

You can apply the same five steps toward accomplishing fitness goals. Set a plan. Get the tools you need—such as new training shoes, headphones, and a planner. Determine when and where you will work out. Add that to your calendar or planner. Decide what workouts you will be doing. Monday could be lower body, Tuesday could be an hour-long walk, Wednesday could be upper body, Thursday could be Pilates, and Friday could be a full body HIIT workout day. Pick a plan and stick to it. If you wake up that day not knowing what you are doing or where you are going, you are likely to fail at creating the habit.

Once you follow through with the plan, cross it off your list, or check the completed box and show yourself how far you've come! There are many habit-tracking calendars you can purchase to see this visually. Once you visually see on the planner or habit tracker how far you've come, you'll want to keep going! Consider incentive and reward systems, such as new workout leggings, when you reach an important milestone.

Accountability

Accountability works in many areas of life. Find an accountability partner such as a friend, parent, significant other, or even a professional.

If you struggle to eat healthy meals, consider hiring a dietitian. If you are struggling with what to do in the gym, consider hiring a trainer in person or virtually. If you are struggling to save money, consider hiring a financial adviser. If you are struggling to stay orderly, consider hiring a professional home organizer. If your finances allow it, having someone help you along the way is beneficial. When your money and someone else's time are on the line, it will typically incentivize you to take the task more seriously.

One time, I wanted to cut out energy drinks because I noticed I was sometimes having up to two per day! *Yikes.* So a friend and I decided for a whole month we would cut them out together. It was tough, but having someone to do it with me and keep me strong sure made it easier. And we actually completed the whole month strong!

Motivation Versus Discipline

Sometimes we think we need to wait for motivation to start a task, but the problem is, we can't rely solely on motivation. Motivation may help you begin the task, but discipline will carry you through it. The more you stay consistent with the small daily habits, the more you will build up this discipline.

Many times I do not want to get out of bed and work out, but I think of how accomplished I will feel after, that I don't want to lose out on the money I already paid for the workout class, and that I am trying to complete five workouts per week. Thinking of the results and benefits more than the emotions and action itself will help you stay motivated. I look at my clothes sitting out for me, change, and go. Sometimes it's a matter of just doing it, even if we don't want to. But I've done this for so long that I don't really think twice about it anymore. Working out is such an ingrained part of my morning routine now that I feel a little off if I don't do it.

Discipline may look like pain, but it's actually growth. There may be things you've done for so long that you just don't think twice about them anymore but they're actually causing you harm. Maybe it's coming home and automatically reaching for a sugary soda, binge-watching a TV show to numb your feelings after a long day, and scrolling on social media for hours before bed. Regardless of what it is, we can get these under control with time and good habits. The more you do the good habits over and over, the easier you will shift into routine and discipline rather than striving for motivation.

It might require cutting out things (permanently or temporarily) that no longer benefit you or aid in your growth. In the Bible, we see how God cuts things off in our lives that harm us. "I am the true vine, and my Father is the gardener. He cuts off every branch in me that bears no fruit, while every branch that does bear fruit he prunes so that it will be even more fruitful" (John 15:1–2). He cuts things off us because he loves us too much to let us wither. It isn't to punish us but rather to prune us for our betterment. Spiritually, there might be habits we do daily that are eating away at our spirit, such as watching overly sexual movies, listening to demeaning songs with cuss words, or using dating apps for temporary affirmations from people. If you can't let go of something, it may have a hold on you. Consider starting with a break from what is holding you back from being the best version of yourself to help it lose control over you.

The process may be tough, painful, and challenging sometimes, but don't quit now! God loves you too much to let you stay in your unhealthy patterns, so he might cut off people, things, and mindsets to help you bear more fruit. Your mind might be the very thing preventing you from finishing strong. If you don't believe you can do it, you won't. You must believe you are fully capable of the things you set out to do! The power of life and death is in the tongue (Proverbs 18:21). Tell yourself that you are more than capable and a conqueror in Christ Jesus (Romans 8:37)!

Ask God and people for help along the way. Sometimes all we need is someone to cheer us on and tell us, "I believe in you!" I know you can do this! Focus on mastering one small task until it becomes a habit you no longer have to rely on motivation to accomplish.

Be Patient with the Process

I know this might feel like a lot of information. You might think, *Well thanks, Jeanine. I'm overwhelmed! I don't even know where to begin.* I get you! Be patient with the process. We are on the path of progress, not perfection. God doesn't expect you to be perfect, so you shouldn't expect that from yourself either. There might be days when you slip up or can't do it. Give yourself a day off, get some rest, take care of yourself, and then the next day, get back on track. I always say this on my podcast: "Don't let yesterday's mistakes stop you from doing the right thing today." Stick to a pace you can sustain. Start small. Don't bite off more than you can chew. And don't let social media make you feel like you are always falling behind. No one does these habits perfectly. If they say they do, they are lying. Everyone has off days, and you can too.

If you fall off the path, you didn't fail—just get right back into it. If I don't get myself to work out in the morning, I make it a plan to go on a walk in the afternoon so I can do at least something active that day. If you become frustrated that you cannot form a habit in a week or a month, here is something that might help. According to a study published in the *European Journal of Social Psychology*, it took their study participants anywhere from eighteen to 254 days to form a regular habit.[3] So don't beat yourself up if it's taking longer than you expected. At least you're trying!

Final Thoughts

I've shared quite a few tips and tricks in this chapter that I hope you find helpful. I know it can feel a bit overwhelming at first, but once you form that habit, you won't even have to think about it anymore. It will become muscle memory.

For me, I create my schedule with the end in mind. I look at what all I need to do before my 9 a.m. workout. If I want to get to my workout on time, I must track backward. To get there on time, make my bed, drink my coffee, reply to texts, make my breakfast, have a quiet time, do my skin care routine, brush my teeth, change into my workout clothes, and drive to my gym, I must wake up no later than 7:30 a.m. That's the actual routine I do every morning. I did not decide one day that I wanted this routine; it formed after adding and subtracting these tasks daily throughout many years. Create a routine that you like and try to follow it until it feels automatic.

Habits have the power to help you overall become happier and more successful holistically. Decide who you want to be, how you will get there, what happens if you slip up, and stay consistent. One day you'll look back on how far you've come and be so proud of yourself that you didn't quit!

MAKE IT REAL IN YOUR LIFE

1. What's a small habit you can start today?
2. What's a negative habit you might need to cut off?
3. Who is someone who can help keep you accountable?
4. What limiting belief do you have that prevents you from achieving your goal?
5. What is something you need to speak daily over yourself in order to believe that you are capable of achieving your goals?

8

Career

How to Be Successful in a God-Glorifying Way

When I was twelve years old, all I wanted was to be the next Hannah Montana. I would sit and watch the show for hours, dreaming of how I too could one day sing and dance on stages. I would perform in my mirror and sing her songs, because the idea of being famous, dressing like a superstar, being on red carpets, and making a lot of money seemed super intriguing to me. The celebrities seemed to enjoy it, so why wouldn't I?

Sadly, I would cry in my purple bedroom because even though I dreamed of this future career, I wasn't sure how it would be possible to get there. In my efforts to achieve it, I looked up online acting auditions, acting agencies, and theaters nearby that I could take classes from. Ya girl was determined! Unfortunately, with me growing up with limited funds and parents who didn't really want their daughter to be influenced by the negative sides of Hollywood, this dream came to an end. I was devastated, yet still hopeful.

One day in 2009, I was scrolling through videos on YouTube and found some girls who created makeup and fashion videos. I was intrigued and began watching hours and hours of their content. I would wait every single week for these girls to upload a new video. I was hooked! After consuming enough of other people's content, I thought to myself, *I can do this too! I like filming stuff, and I have some tips I could share!* And thus was the creation of my own YouTube channel. In February 2010, I started my channel named "Jeaninegirl94." Kind of embarrassing, right? I guess I just really had to let people know I was a girl born in 1994.

The start of this YouTube channel led to my current career as a podcast host, YouTuber, Bible teacher, social media influencer, speaker, and now author! By consistently posting online, collaborating with other well-known influencers, and trying to put out content to help people, I grew my collective following to more than 2.7 million followers. I don't think twelve-year-old Jeanine in her purple bedroom would have ever imagined that! So even though I didn't become a superstar (RIP), I do something now that I love even more and that I wholeheartedly believe is a gift from God. I am able to still speak to many people on stages, help people through my content, use my gifts and creativity, all while being my own boss. I may not have ever known that uploading silly videos to YouTube would one day transpire into my career now, but God did. Looking back, I'm happy I didn't become a superstar. I think I would have been unfilled, considering how damaging Hollywood can be to some people. I'm grateful my path was derailed. My favorite thing about my job now is that I get to help people, connect with women all around the world, and genuinely see lives changed for the Kingdom.

I share this story to show you that sometimes God puts dreams in our hearts for a reason, even though we may not know what to do with them. But if it's from the Lord, he will prepare a way. Sometimes these dreams don't turn out exactly like we expected, but if there's a God-given desire in us, he will open the doors to allow it to happen. Maybe there's a dream in your heart and you're wondering, *How will I ever get there?* Trust me, if it's from the Lord, he will direct you. Proverbs 16:9 says, "In their hearts humans plan their course, but the LORD establishes their steps."

For many of you, finding your purpose feels like a daunting question mark that lingers over your head. You know it's there, but you just don't know what it is. Many people DM me and ask, "How do I find my purpose? I don't know what I want to do with my life." You might just be getting out of college and feel beyond overwhelmed. You might have a degree and still have no clue what you are doing with your life. Or maybe you don't have a degree and didn't go to college, which is also fine, but you may still feel stuck. There are so many options out there—but also so much pressure from society, our peers, parents, social media, and even ourselves to figure it out.

Everyone wants to be successful and achieve something in their life. Sometimes people feel like they're not doing anything important if it doesn't resemble the achievements of their friends or someone they see online. We want to do something that lights us up and makes us feel fulfilled, but we just don't know how to get there. Some of us put too much pressure on ourselves to know what we want or ought to do, when that's simply not always realistic. Sometimes we don't find that out until later in life, and that is okay. Renowned fashion designer Vera Wang didn't design her first dress until she was forty. Henry Ford was forty-five when he created the revolutionary Model T car in 1908. Harry Bernstein wrote many books that were rejected before publishing his first successful book at age ninety-six. And even Jesus didn't begin his ministry until he was thirty! So give yourself a break in desiring to have it all figured out right now. It will come with patience, persistence, and prayer. Good things take time. God-ordained things take time. Preparation in private for your purpose is a process you can't rush. The preparation will be important to make sure you are ready for the calling. Here are some starter questions to help you find your purpose.

What are you currently interested in?

Often the things people genuinely love to do become their job or passion. Can that turn into a career somehow? Can you find a solution to a common problem?

I have a friend who loves to work out but has struggled with food addictions and poor eating habits. She is now a personal trainer and has started a program with the goal of helping women to overcome insecurities and disordered eating and to heal from body shame, using what she's learned in her own story. Using your passions to help other people and make money is often a route to success. So look at your story and consider what you've experienced that could help someone else.

Have people ever told you that you're gifted in a particular area?

God made you *you* for a reason. This is your opportunity to capitalize on your gifts as a stepping-stone into your career. Often, they are the things people already affirm in you. People told me at a young age that they thought I would be an amazing speaker one day and good on camera, and now that's a massive part of my job!

Maybe you're gifted at playing piano. Can you teach music to kids? Are you good with numbers? Maybe you'd make a great accountant. Maybe you're super stylish and love fashion. Can you help people reorganize their closets or style them for events? The possibilities are endless!

Are you currently using your job to bless others?

Sometimes, I think people have an escapism mentality that says, *If only I get there, things will be better.* Why not try thinking instead, *How can I use my current situation and job to be a blessing and steward this well now?* You never know how your current job or situation can propel you into the next one by stewarding what you have now with excellence. Sometimes people want to skip from job to job in hopes that the next will finally solve their problems, when that may not be true. The best thing you can do is master what you have now, bless the people there, and see what other doors God opens. After all, your current employer may not want to give you a recommendation for the next opportunity that comes your way if you've made it clear you don't want to be there and can't be depended on for quality work.

Just because your job may not pay a lot of money or be deemed as important doesn't mean it isn't. You get to decide that and make the best of it. If you're a babysitter, be the best babysitter ever—teach the kids something, love them well, show them the heart of Jesus, and serve the parents well. Even if others may look at you like you're less successful for being a babysitter, you can still be purposeful and on mission with that role and make a difference.

Being on a mission and finding your purpose involves finding meaning in everything you do. It's a mindset shift. It's not looking for a job title, a particular income level, or a certain status; it's being purposeful with everything you have now. If you don't appreciate the little now, you won't appreciate the big later. Often purpose comes from seeing a need, filling it, and making people smile. Maybe you have a coworker who's going through a hard time. Bring them flowers or a homemade pie or their favorite coffee order. It's the little things that truly make people's day. One of my friends went to lunch with his boss before leaving his job, and he encouraged his boss in something he was struggling with, and his boss told him the day he left, "Even though you worked here a short time, you have greatly impacted my life in ways you'll never even know." *Wow*, right? Purpose is found in people!

Finding purpose in life is actually simpler than you think. The Bible gives us instructions on what to do. The Pharisees asked Jesus in Matthew 22:34–40 what the greatest commandment of all time was, and Jesus responded: "'Love the Lord your God with all your heart and with all your soul and with all your mind.' This is the first and greatest commandment. And the second is like it: 'Love your neighbor as yourself.' All the Law and the Prophets hang on these two commandments." Here we find an incredible purpose no matter our job title or our to-do list. Regardless of your position, how can you love God and love people every single day? This perspective helps uncomplicate our worries and wonders.

This is what helped me find purpose in my job. Throughout my social media journey, I struggled quite a bit. I thought to myself, *This just isn't for me anymore.* I couldn't handle the pressure and belittling comments. I often felt unfulfilled posting things that seemed superficial at times. Once the Lord grabbed ahold of my heart, everything changed.

After asking him for his will in my job, I felt more purposeful. Every day when I spent time with the Lord, I fell more in love with him, and that helped me love others. And that love led me to begin sharing more of my story online in hopes it would help other women and set them free too—free from shame, from poor dating habits, from addictions, and into a fulfilling, joyful, God-filled life.

Falling in love with Jesus helped me love others more. It opened my eyes to see how much need the world has, how many people are hurting and struggling. I began to use my platform to share not only fashion and lifestyle tips but spiritual and mental advice that was genuinely setting people free through the power of Jesus. This led me to absolutely love my job, because I now get to use something I already enjoy to help others. All this to say, you can find purpose in anything you do if you ask, "How does this help me love God and others more?" Purpose is everywhere if we look hard enough.

Having dreams, goals, and ambitions isn't a bad thing. There is nothing wrong with wanting to be successful, but it's what you do with success that matters. We must check our intentions. If you're pursuing a dream, ask yourself why and who it's for. Is this career choice simply to make others happy? Are you only doing it out of fear of disappointing someone? Or is this dream something you genuinely desire and can see blessing others too? Maybe you don't know the answer to either yet, and that's okay. There is no pressure from me! I only want to challenge you to seek the Lord as you seek your dreams.

Seeking the Lord in Your Purpose

When seeking out a dream, I believe it's always important to ask the Lord for his guidance and will in the whole process. Even if you don't know quite yet what that endeavor might be, asking the Lord for his will and plan over yours will always be beneficial. We are called to be bold and take a leap of faith, even if we don't know where we're going yet, and trust that God will direct us (and redirect us if we get off track). Submitting to the Lord your dreams and desires will always go well for you. He wants to be involved because he cares for you. Psalm 37:4 says, "Take delight in the Lord, and he will give you the desires of your heart," and Matthew 6:33 (NLT) says, "Seek the Kingdom of God above all else, and live righteously, and he will give you everything you need."

These verses tell us that the Lord will provide everything we need as we seek him. As we delight in him. As we follow him. As we learn to love him and his ways. This should help take some weight off your shoulders, because now you know your success is not based only on you anymore. I'm not saying sit on the couch and be lazy because God will provide everything, but I'm asking you to partner with God on finding your passion, and trust that he will guide you.

Maybe you feel nervous because it's scary taking a leap of faith. Or maybe you feel frustrated because you don't know how to get there. Or maybe you don't feel equipped or qualified because what you desire seems too big or impossible. You aren't the first person to feel that way! Reading the story of Moses in the book of Exodus proves that people have been overwhelmed by God's purpose for their lives for centuries! Moses was a prophet, a leader, and the establisher of the first laws and structure for the Israelite religion and society. God knew that Moses would struggle with fear in the call set before him:

> Moses said to the Lord, "Pardon your servant, Lord. I have never been eloquent, neither in the past nor since you have spoken to your servant. I am slow of speech and tongue."

113

The LORD said to him, "Who gave human beings their mouths? Who makes them deaf or mute? Who gives them sight or makes them blind? Is it not I, the LORD? Now go; I will help you speak and will teach you what to say."

But Moses said, "Pardon your servant, Lord. Please send someone else."

Exodus 4:10–13

Moses was scared of the calling God put on his life. He made excuses, claiming he wasn't qualified. He even asked the Lord to send someone else! But God told him, "*I will help you.*" If one of the most important men in the Bible was scared of his calling and God still helped him, how much more grace is there for us in ours?

So rest assured, my friends, he's got you. Continue to ask the Lord to show you what to do, how to do it, who to do it with, and when to do it, and he will. "Commit to the Lord whatever you do, and he will establish your plans" (Proverbs 16:3). Don't forget to continue to seek him even after you get the dream or the desire.

Work Ethic

Here's the truth—pursuing your passions and dreams is going to require hard work. We want the results without the required effort. We want to skip to the good part, where we have the finances, the dream career, the house, or the number of followers we desire, but that's not reality. I think there is a balance between trusting the Lord with your dreams and career and still putting in the work. The Bible states more than once that hard work pays off. Don't get me wrong. I'm not encouraging you to fall into a toxic, hustle-culture mentality, but I am saying that God rewards hard work when we're also faithfully following him. Proverbs 14:23 says, "All hard work brings a profit, but mere talk leads only to poverty," and Proverbs 13:4 says, "A sluggard's appetite is never filled, but the desires of the diligent are fully satisfied."

Sometimes the initial jobs you do until your dream job comes to pass won't always be the most fulfilling. People are usually searching for fulfillment and keep passing up jobs until they find it, but sometimes we don't find it until way later in our life. We don't want to wish away our lives, waiting for what we think will fulfill us. We need to put our heads down, make a purpose where we are planted, and use the current job as a stepping-stone to the next. Make the best of every season!

Even when you do have your dream job, some tasks will feel mundane or boring; that's why discipline and work ethic matter—things you can practice right now. Working hard and diligently, even though you may not enjoy it, builds character in a way that you can only get by going through it. Over the years I pursued my current position, there were many things I dreaded doing. But I thought of where I wanted to be and of how stewarding the little I had currently would allow God to entrust me with more later (see Luke 16:10). Be faithful with the little, and God will bless you with the much.

Every successful person you've seen has had to put in years of time, money, sleepless nights, effort, and consistency. Nothing happens overnight (unless you win the lottery), but often the very people you admire who seem to have it all together are actually struggling like you. They might have been tempted to jump ship. Or they may have been discouraged by people who didn't understand their dream and said to themselves, "Why are you wasting your time on this? Give up!" The journey typically doesn't look glamorous, but it's worth it when you see the final result! Whatever the case may be, hard work works. So never compare your first proposal to someone else's finished product.

Money and Integrity

While pursuing your passions, never forsake integrity and honest work for a get-rich-quick scheme. Money made in a deceitful and corrupt way won't go well for you. "A hard worker has plenty of food, but a person who *chases* fantasies ends up in poverty. The *trustworthy* person will get a rich reward, but a person who wants quick riches will get into *trouble*" (Proverbs 28:19–20 NLT, emphasis added).

I bring this up because I know the temptation of the world to buy followers, make deals under the table, or compromise your morals in order to get money quickly—but it's simply not worth it. Just like God honors hard work, he also honors integrity and trustworthiness. Proverbs 13:11 says, "Dishonest money dwindles away, but whoever gathers money little by little makes it grow," and Proverbs 28:18 (ESV) says, "Whoever walks in integrity will be delivered, but he who is crooked in his ways will suddenly fall." Honest, hard-earned money is much more rewarding than quick, crookedly earned money. It will keep your conscience clear and your passions protected.

Whatever you do, do it for the Lord. Honor him with your work. When you have those days of feeling like you want to slack off, remind yourself that you are working for the Lord and honoring him, which produces a greater reward. "Whatever you do, work at it with all your heart, as working for the Lord, not for human masters, since you know that you will receive an inheritance from the Lord as a reward. It is the Lord Christ you are serving" (Colossians 3:23–24).

I also want to gently remind you of the danger of making money and your career into an idol. While it's not inherently bad to be rich or desire financial stability, the problem is when we think it will bring us full joy and satisfaction. This false belief can lead us down some very dangerous paths. Additionally, the love of money can make us more selfish, arrogant, haughty, or prideful. "For the love of money is a root of all kinds of evil. Some people, eager for money, have wandered from the faith and pierced themselves with many griefs" (1 Timothy 6:10). This verse isn't saying that having money is bad or wrong, but it's the *love* of money that becomes dangerous. People wander from their faith and leave God behind in their pursuit of money and pleasures because they think they're good now that they've become successful. They replace the Creator with his creation (see Romans 1:25).

Never let money become your God. There's a saying I hear often: "The more money, the more problems." I think that can be so true. I've seen money do some very destructive things to families, best friends, influencers, celebrities, and many others. Keep a humble, serving, teachable heart, no matter how successful you get.

Be generous with your money. Share and be faithful with what you have now. Be grateful for what God has given you. Give God glory with it all. And be faithful with each season. Success isn't wrong, just be mindful of what you do with it. Will your success benefit only you—or will you use it to help others too?

People Along the Way

To close out this chapter, let's talk about the importance of people along the way. When I was beginning my career, I couldn't have made it on my own—and neither can you. It's important to be willing to ask for help, because odds are, you will need it. Culture pushes this toxic, self-sufficient mentality that "You only need yourself," but that's a lie. Remember when I talked about the importance of friendships and community in chapter 4? Community is necessary for the health and success of your career as well. If you want to go far, you can't go alone.

Ask wise people for advice, meet with someone who has achieved the success that you want and ask them questions, or start a business with someone you trust. Have people vet and speak into your business plan—and be willing to take the feedback. Fun fact: I almost quit YouTube, even though I felt the Lord was in it. I was so close to quitting, until I reached out to another YouTube friend and sought counsel. Thankfully, she encouraged me to keep going and gave me some pointers on what to do next. If it weren't for her, I'm not sure where I would be. Having people along the way encourage you and believe in you is so vital and truly life changing.

Sometimes your God-given dreams may look odd to the world. Your parents may not get it—or friends or coworkers—but keep going. If God has placed a dream in your heart, people don't always need to understand it. It's between you and God. The right people, whom God has placed in your life, will understand it and support you. It doesn't need to make sense to all the people, just the right people. Focus on who you're trying to reach and keep going. My content may not be for everyone, but it's for someone. It's the same for you, my friend. I believe in you, and I am rooting for you!

MAKE IT REAL IN YOUR LIFE

1. What is your God-given dream?
2. What gifts has God given you that could turn into something bigger?
3. What one small step can you make right now to move closer to your dream?
4. Who do you need to reach out to for help?
5. Who is your dream for?

9

Decisions

How to Hear from God and Make Wise Choices

While living alone for over a year during the pandemic, I struggled with loneliness and feeling homesick. I contemplated moving back home to Dallas, but I just didn't feel ready yet. I had it set in my mind that I was going to live in LA for at least four years. I had already done three, so why not finish out the fourth? I loved my life there! I had a great church, community, and home. But the pandemic drastically changed my lifestyle and my original reason for moving there. I kept feeling this constant *ping* in my spirit from the Lord that my time was wrapping up there. It was like this constant tap on my shoulder that I tried my best to brush off, but it kept resurfacing.

I didn't want to continue living alone, so I tried living with my friend Shelby, but she had already found another option. Then my best friend, Madi, was considering moving to LA to live with me, but after a lot of prayer, she felt the Lord tell her that she was supposed to move to Dallas. Every apartment I toured just didn't feel right or didn't have the right features I was looking for. All the doors to staying in LA started to feel like they were shutting on me. I was super sad, but I was determined to stay. I even told Madi, "I just don't want to move back. I'm not ready yet. Dallas feels like going backward in life."

On September 20, 2020, I went back to Dallas to see my family, and I felt the Lord clearly tell me during my flight, "Your season of living alone is over, you will move back to Dallas, and you will meet your husband in Texas." I sat there shocked. *Was that me or was that God?* I jotted it down in my journal with some question marks and told the Lord, "If this is from you, please confirm it." As I was landing in Dallas and saw the city's skyline, I began to tear up and felt so much peace. I was home.

Throughout the weekend, I felt the Lord remind me why this city was going to be good for me again. I immediately called Madi after that visit and told her, "I think I'm supposed to move back to Dallas." She freaked out and said, "J, I just got done fasting and praying that you would change your mind, and you did!" We both screamed and said, "We are moving to Dallas!"

After that weekend, I set out on my journey of moving back to Dallas and buying a home. Leaving LA was difficult. It came with a lot of tears, hard decisions, prayers, and bittersweet good-byes to the friends and life I had there—yet the Lord was still very much in it. Little did I know that moving back to Dallas and living with Madi was going to be the biggest blessing ever; it was anything but going backward. Making that decision wasn't easy and came with a lot of fear and processing, but the Lord prepared a way and blessed it. It was the best thing to happen to me. That date, September twentieth, was prophesied over me in 2019 as an important date, but I just didn't know what for. God spoke to me on that specific day, and now those three things all ended up coming true. As I am revising this book, I am now soon to marry an incredible, godly man I met two years into living back in Texas. God is so faithful to fulfill his words to us when he speaks! But how does God speak? Let's talk about it.

In this chapter I want to talk about the logistics of making decisions and deciphering whether you are hearing from the Lord or not. Maybe you're in a situation similar to mine, trying to decide between two good options. Life will always present us with decisions, but how do you know you are making the right one? I know it isn't easy. Sometimes it feels like we are waiting forever for God to give us an answer, and sometimes he doesn't. What now? I'm going to help you know how God speaks and how to make wise decisions when you feel stuck!

How Does God Speak?

Through God's Word

God can speak to us in many ways, but most often he speaks to us through his Word. You might think, *Isn't that book a bit antiquated and only for the people of the past?* Yes, the Bible was written more than two thousand years ago, but the truths in Scripture are still very much applicable today. Stories about the people who were alive around Jesus's time, and even before, teach us important lessons today. The Bible was written with God, knowing that his Word would live on forever and that we still need it today for whatever we face.

The Bible says in Hebrews 4:12, "For the word of God is alive and active. Sharper than any double-edged sword, it penetrates even to dividing soul and spirit, joints and marrow; it judges the thoughts and attitudes of the heart." This means we can refer to it every day and find help in our current circumstances. This is such great news! Before any other way that God speaks, he speaks through his Word. Psalm 119:105 says, "Your word is a lamp for my feet, a light on my path." His Word is a guide for us, lighting the best path when we're trying to discern what to do. This might come from examples of people's stories recorded in Scripture, or by seeing more of God's character and how he sounds when he speaks to us. It might be that while or after reading the Bible you feel a nudge or a peace about one direction or another. So when you're trying to decide on what to do, start with the Bible.

The Bible can be a bit overwhelming, I know, but refer to chapter 1 again on where to begin reading. The book of Proverbs has hundreds of quick, wise sayings that will give you a ton of insight, wisdom, and instructions for decisions you're making. When making a decision, it's always wise to ask yourself, "Does this decision align with God's Word?" Because God will never tell you to do something that goes against his Word. Never. He's not going to be wishy-washy on what he's written to try to confuse you (1 Corinthians 14:33). His truths are consistent throughout Scripture and in our lives today, which should be a relief for you, because it's the one thing that is consistent and stable when society and trends are everchanging.

It can be hard to know God's will for our current situations, since the Bible doesn't talk about what college to choose, whom to marry, or what job to take. But we can apply biblical principles to our situations, since God's Word and character remain the same. So even though God may not always tell you exactly what you should do, you can trust that if you seek him, he's not going to let you fall (Psalm 37:23–24).

Through God's people

God speaks through his people, and it will always be wise to consult godly people when making decisions. Someone may have past experience, more biblical knowledge, or more wisdom than you to help you know what to do. Proverbs 12:15 (ESV) says, "The way of a fool is right in his own eyes, but a wise man listens to advice." Wisdom is listening to advice and not always thinking your way is right.

God may also give knowledge to someone else before he gives it to you regarding something you're going through. Through the gifts of prophecy or knowledge, God can speak through someone else to tell you something he wants you to know. However, this also needs to be aligned with Scripture and be tested. A proclamation from someone about what you should do isn't something to blindly take at face value. Instead, write it down, store it away, and see if the Lord eventually confirms it in your own spirit and life. If it's from God, it will come to pass. If it doesn't, trust that God can still speak to you, regardless of what this person told you.

Countless times in my life, people have spoken something to me that was spot on, and I knew it was from the Lord. For example, one time I was moments away from signing a lease in LA for an apartment I wasn't all that excited about, and the landlord was rushing me with a time constraint. I felt very confused, and suddenly I got a text from my friend Sarah, who had no idea what I was going through, that said, "I felt the Lord tell me that there is some contract you are about to sign that you shouldn't." My mouth dropped wide open. I was so shocked! I was moments away from signing that lease out of fear that I wouldn't find something else, but I didn't end up doing it, and it was truly for the best. A couple days later, I found an apartment that was perfect for me! This type of prophecy may not happen often, but when it does, it's God showing us that he sees us, is looking out for us, and will speak to us through his people with the Holy Spirit. Remember: people are not God, and their insight is not always the final answer, but they sure can help you discern God's voice. Always submit what someone says to you back to the Lord and ask him to show you if it's his plan or not. If it's from the Lord, it will happen in his timing.

Who you seek advice from matters just as much as deciding to seek counsel. The two should go hand in hand. Who you get advice from will determine how healthy and wise the advice actually is. When seeking advice, you'll want to go through a filter of qualities to determine if a person is, in fact, "good counsel." Generally, you'll want to seek advice from someone who knows the Bible and applies it well. How do you know this? You see how they live and what fruit is growing in their life. Is this:

- Someone who knows the Bible and what it says?
- Someone who has a blessed and fruitful life by following God's Word?

- Someone you respect?
- Someone others respect?
- Someone who has good intentions toward you?
- Someone who has experience in the matter you are asking about?

The specific issue might also determine who you ask. If you're needing relationship help, you might go to an older married couple and ask them to help you process through a dating relationship you are struggling with. If you need financial help, you might seek out someone you know is successful or manages money for a living and ask them for advice. If you are struggling mentally, you might seek out a counselor or someone who has overcome some of the same struggles you're having. Don't take advice from someone who isn't where you'd want to be. For instance, avoid taking financial advice from someone who frivolously spends their money, and avoid asking someone for dating advice who doesn't seem to have a healthy pattern of dating. If you aren't a Christian, then you might not know what biblical advice looks like. But generally, seek out someone who is where you want to be or has overcome what you want to overcome.

Through prayer, dreams, and visions

God can speak to you directly as well through your prayer time, dreams, and even visions. Maybe some of this information is a bit new and intimidating for you, but it is all very real and possible. The Bible even tells us in 1 Corinthians 14:1 (ESV) to earnestly desire the gifts: "Pursue love, and earnestly desire the spiritual gifts, especially that you may prophesy." We just have to ask for it, and if it's in his will, he'll give those gifts to us. Sometimes when you are praying, a phrase or a verse that you didn't know on your own or had long forgotten about might pop into your head. For example, one night after my roommate had moved out and I was single, sad, and living alone again, I was lying in bed feeling lonely and nervous. I said,

"God, I feel scared," and I instantly heard *Joshua 1:9* in my head. It wasn't an audible voice, but a gentle, quiet voice. I quickly looked up that verse in my Bible app, and to my surprise, it was exactly what I needed! Joshua 1:9 says, "Have I not commanded you? Be strong and courageous. Do not be afraid; do not be discouraged, for the LORD your God will be with you wherever you go." I was beyond encouraged. I knew it was the Lord letting me know he was with me. He still speaks to us, and it's so sweet when he does.

Another way I have seen God speak is through dreams and visions. I'm not saying you're a fortune-teller, but I am saying that God is in the supernatural. Both prophetic dreams and visions are mentioned in the Bible and have been used several times by the Lord to speak to his people. Acts 2:17 says, "In the last days, God says, I will pour out my Spirit on all people. Your sons and daughters will prophesy, your young men will see visions, your old men will dream dreams."

I know sometimes our dreams can be a bit weird, like flying through the sky on a unicorn, but sometimes you may have ones that just seem oddly specific, and you feel something is different once you wake up. It may be a dream warning you about someone or something, or perhaps a dream to convict you about something you are doing, or simply a dream about something God just wants to show you about a current situation you are facing. Whatever the case may be, write your dream down, pray over it, and ask the Lord to show you what it means. These too should line up with Scripture.

Visions can be like a little movie or picture in your head about something God wants to show you. I have two friends who are gifted with dreams and visions, and in April 2019, one of them told me of a vision they had where I would be speaking on stages one day, be in rooms with pastors and leaders, and would have a book on Christian bookshelves. At that time, I never did speaking engagements, was barely sharing my faith online, and didn't even have an idea for a book. It is so amazing to see this all come to fruition, but at the time, I didn't fully believe it. I screenshotted the message and saved it to see if the Lord would make it come true, and eventually, all three did! If someone does that to you, see if it resonates with God's Word and feels right in your spirit. Write it down and ask the Lord to show you if it's for you or not. He will!

If this is all new for you, know that you too have access to these gifts through the Holy Spirit. Know that they are not essential for your salvation, they do not make you a superhero, and they do not make you better than anyone else, but they are a free gift God can give you to guide and encourage you and others. You may not get these particular gifts immediately, or at all, but it doesn't change the fact that God still speaks to us today. Above all, the Bible is the most important tool to lean on. It will never fail us and is still relevant for us today. Whether through his Word, his people, or these gifts, God wants to lead you through whatever you're experiencing. He says in Jeremiah 33:3 (ESV), "Call to me and I will answer you, and will tell you great and hidden things that you have not known." Pray for God to speak to you, because he wants to!

Deciphering God's Voice While Making a Decision

You will inevitably be at a crossroads at some point. Two paths are possible, both good options, and you just don't know what to do. Maybe you're deciding between two jobs. One provides more money but requires you to move away from home and leave your friends and family behind. The other is way less money but could eventually lead to a better position later down the road, and you get to stay in your current community. Which one do you take? Sometimes we know the answer right away, but other times, nothing makes sense. Don't feel scared if you're not sure what to do. The Bible says that God is the one who directs our steps, even if we plan them out (Proverbs 16:9). So rest assured that even in your free will, he will continue to bless your path in whatever you take if you're obedient to him in the process. I think some of us are so scared to step outside of God's will that we do nothing at all. Sometimes we're called to just make the first step and trust that God will show us if we get off track.

Whether you're hearing God's voice and direction through prayer, reading Scripture, other people's insight, or personal revelation through dreams or visions, it's wise to examine those messages before moving forward. Let's talk about specific questions we can ask to help us make a good, godly decision.

What does the Bible say?

This is the most important question to ask. As I said in the beginning, God's Word is always something we should refer to in anything we do. The more you read the Word and know it, the easier it will be to make godly, wise decisions. Is there a verse that can speak to the exact situation you're going through? Maybe you're deciding if you should party at the bars because your friends are pressuring you. (I get it, this was me in college.) Reading the verse that says, "Do not get drunk on wine, which leads to debauchery. Instead, be filled with the Spirit" (Ephesians 5:18), could be helpful. God will not contradict his Word. Ever. If you are thinking, *It's just one night of fun, why not?* that is not God you are hearing. That is either your flesh or Satan whispering lies—and we know this because it contradicts what we read in Scripture. This is why it's so important to funnel your decisions and thoughts through the Word—the compass of the truth.

Regardless of what decision you're facing, pause and ask yourself, *What would God say about this?* Don't feel ashamed if you need to Google verses that speak to your situation. I do it all the time! As long as you find the verses and let them guide you, you will be better off than just trusting yourself.

Which path will draw me closer to Jesus?

When there are two or three paths you are deciding between, a good question to ask is, *Will this draw me closer to Jesus?* If moving to a new city to find a better godly community or ending a relationship with someone who has pulled you away from God will result in you becoming closer to God, then those might be good reasons to make those decisions. One option, however, may be so blatantly harmful to you and your faith, and it will be a simple choice. You must be willing to take time and not make an irrational decision. A big decision should never be made on a whim, based purely on emotions or to escape something you haven't fully worked through. Weigh the pros and cons of each, and ultimately let the one that pushes you closer to Jesus win. You cannot go wrong with this thinking. Wisdom in decision-making says to be slow, thoughtful, and prayerful. Don't do something you will regret later out of impulse or insecurities.

What does godly wisdom say through community?

When you are facing a difficult or complicated decision, never be wise in your own sight, as Isaiah 5:21 says, "Woe to those who are wise in their own eyes and clever in their own sight." Bring all the information you have to someone you trust and have them walk through each option with you. Have them ask you challenging questions regarding each option:

1. What have you heard the Lord say so far?
2. Will this option honor God and bring you closer to him? If so, how?
3. What will you do once you get that option?
4. Will this option be truly beneficial for you?
5. Is there a secret, ulterior motive as to why you want it?
6. What are the pros and cons of this decision?

Sometimes as we are making decisions, something in our subconscious desires a certain result more than we'd like to admit, which may lead to potential poor decision-making. It's helpful to have someone ask you more challenging questions and dive deep into the "why." In isolation, we often default to our subconscious desires, which may not be the most godly, beneficial choice.

Trusted community is everything in decision-making. Before buying a car, moving, picking a college, marrying someone, choosing a roommate, leaving or starting a job, buying an expensive purchase, choosing a church, or going on a date, bring others into the decision-making process. They may be the very reason you avoid something harmful!

What makes the most sense?

Sometimes we stress out a little too much over a decision, when we just need to look at the hard facts to discover what makes the most sense. We can be so fearful that we will make the wrong choice or step outside God's will that we become paralyzed. If something is the most beneficial choice and others agree, and you feel good about it, then go for it! For example, if a college is offering you scholarships, it has a good program for what you want to do, it has a solid Christian ministry, and it's not too far away from home, it's probably the right choice over a college that costs too much money, is too far away, and isn't somewhere you really want to be anyway. I don't think we need to overcomplicate all of our decisions. Use your best godly judgment, pray about it, and if you feel peace in the decision, do it!

Sometimes God is already laying it out plainly for us by shutting one door and opening another. So look for doors opening and closing, because those can often be indicators that God is highlighting a certain path.

When I was deciding whether to move home to Dallas, I felt the Lord was shutting doors in LA. In addition, my feelings about LA began to change, my parents encouraged me to return home, and Madi wanted to move to my hometown. It all just seemed to fit too perfectly for it not to make sense! If I had stayed in LA, God could have still blessed it, but I do think my life would look immensely different today.

Don't overcomplicate simple decisions and get analysis paralysis. Sometimes we know the answer already and all the signs are pointing that direction, but we're fearful to step into the unknown. Take a step of faith and trust that God cares too much for you to let you fall. Sometimes we need to release the pressure we put on ourselves to be perfect, make the best decision we can, and trust that if we walk with God and people around us, we will be guided in our next endeavor.

You can't mess up!

My favorite point of all is this—you can't mess this up, my friend! If you are not living in willful disobedience to God, are walking with community, and are surrendered to him, he will always direct or redirect your steps. Sometimes God won't give you the answer because both options are good and you just need to make a choice. We beg God for peace in our decisions, since God often does show us what to do by giving us peace or a lack of peace, but sometimes we hear silence. If you hear silence and don't feel an overwhelming sense of lack of peace, you're going to be okay. Pray more for an overwhelming disruption of peace, since that will be a more accurate meter in decision-making. A disruption of peace may be God trying to wake you up or show you something that you should run away from. God is called the God of peace (Romans 15:33), and he lives within you. So with the Holy Spirit inside you, if you feel his peace about a choice and you seek him, you can't mess up. "And your ears shall hear a word behind you, saying, 'This is the way, walk in it,' when you turn to the right or when you turn to the left" (Isaiah 30:21 ESV). We can all let out a sigh of relief now!

I pray this chapter is a helpful tool for you to return to as you navigate the challenges of big decisions in life. Hopefully decision-making feels less daunting now and you have more wisdom on what to do next. You are well on your way to happier and healthier life as you seek him in the big and small moments. Trust the Holy Spirit inside you!

MAKE IT REAL IN YOUR LIFE

1. How have I seen God show up in my decisions before?
2. Have you heard the voice of God before? If so, how?
3. What decision are you facing now, and how can you apply the advice in this chapter?
4. Who in your life can you seek wise advice from?
5. What questions have you not considered seriously in the past that you will now going forward?

10

Secrets

How Honesty and Vulnerability Help You Grow

Not to be dramatic, but my senior year of college was probably the worst time of my life. I was balancing my communications major, business minor, cheerleading, full-time social media job, and a long-distance relationship. This was also when I began to live alone for my first time, since my sisters and all my close friends had already graduated. I was beyond isolated and lonely. I was still trying to seek Christ in my life but felt distant from him. My two-and-half-year relationship had become toxic, abusive, and manipulative. It wasn't always unhealthy, but somehow it grew to be my worst nightmare. I didn't realize how bad it was until everything exploded in my face.

Being alone, unhealthy, and lukewarm in my faith, I made the unwise decision to elope with my then-boyfriend, which means we legally got married without anyone's knowledge. It was a day I'll never forget. Despite my efforts to wait until marriage for sex, I unfortunately didn't with this man, which caused even more feelings of shame and like I *had* to stay with him. After almost two months of feeling pressured into this life-altering decision, my weak, young, naive self caved. As we pulled up to the courthouse to get the marriage certificate, this sinking feeling began to overwhelm me. I knew this was wrong. I felt an achy pain in my stomach. I knew I was making a mistake, but he begged me to go inside and said he would pay for it if I just did it. I was made to believe that if I wasn't with him, my career would tank without him and no one would ever want me—the most terrifying feeling.

We signed the papers, and instantly regret came over me. He celebrated while I panicked. *What did I just do? I'm stuck in this now.* I began to feel anxiety throughout my body as he drank in celebration. Shortly into this so-called marriage, the truth began to come out. The man I had married was not the man I once knew. Lies and secrets of what he'd been doing the previous six months without my knowledge began to unravel. Who knew someone who said they *loved* you could lie to you so much? I felt trapped, but I told myself I was committed. I made this decision, so I felt I had to live with it. Nervous for my future, I finally told my sister what had happened. I saw the look of strong concern on her face, and she said, "Jeanine, this isn't right . . . you guys need help. This isn't healthy." I knew it wasn't. I wanted out. I wanted help. But he didn't. It takes two people to get healthy, but only one wanted it.

Within a week of that conversation, all my family learned about what I'd done and tried to help me. It was the scariest feeling, exposing my deep, dark secret to them. My dad strongly disapproved of the marriage and of the guy, and he told me to get an annulment, meaning to legally undo the marriage. Hearing the word *annulment* was the first time I felt peace in over a month and a half. I knew it was what I had to do. I tried to do it respectfully, but it was the last thing my ex wanted. I remember him telling me, "If you get an annulment from me, I will make your life a living hell." And he did. The next couple months consisted of him posting deceitful videos online about me and sending them to all my friends and followers, him trying to secretly steal money from me, calling the cops on me, threatening to take everything I had worked for, screaming in my face, and treating me like I was dispensable and unvaluable. I wasn't perfect either in this relationship by any means, but I was scared. Any self-esteem and happiness I had went completely out the window. I lost so much weight due to my anxiety, and I wanted to end my life due to how much pain, embarrassment, and shame I felt trapped in. I would never wish this feeling on anyone.

But after many traumatic months of arguing with him and me begging God on my knees for help, we came to an agreement and legally separated. After it all ended, I fell on my face and thanked God for his mercy and grace over my life and future. I didn't feel I deserved a second chance, but God was gracious to me.

Welcome to my story. It's a story I haven't shared much until this moment because I wasn't ready and was still filled with shame, but I'm ready now. Since then, I have made drastic changes in my life so that will never happen again, and I vowed to walk with wisdom and obedience with the Lord in all I do. I share this story to show you that we all have our pasts and secrets, and I pray that mine will help someone else become free from the same situation. Even though our stories may not be what we would have chosen for ourselves, they somehow still serve a purpose. Some of us got cards dealt to us that may seem unfair or unjust, and some of us dealt ourselves the cards with the choices we made.

But it doesn't mean all hope is lost. Even though you may have something in your past that you might deem irreparable or shameful, I believe there's something so powerful in how God can redeem that. That's a story worth sharing and hearing. Even if your story is hard and painful, like mine was, God can use it for something even greater. Our stories are never wasted.

Secrets, Sins, and Struggles

Here's the thing with our secrets, sins, or struggles: everyone has them, even if they don't admit it. Some may share them louder than others (heck, I just shared mine in a book for many to read), but you'd be surprised at the things you'd discover if you sat down with someone you think you know. Plenty of people have probably done the same thing as you. Now, this isn't a pass for you to keep on doing it, but rather to help you know that you are not alone in feeling the way you do. For some of you, there are things you've been carrying for years that you *swore* you'd never tell anyone. You might think, *Absolutely no one can know this, or they will judge me and think I'm a horrible person.* I get it. I carried that around for many years, but at some point, you've got to uncover the truth and release it to find freedom. Sometimes we don't open up about our struggles for the following reasons:

- You think no one else deals with it.
- You're too embarrassed and ashamed to admit it.
- You're not ready to let go if it yet.
- You're afraid of what people might think.
- You like the sin or struggle you're in because it's familiar and comforting.
- It's not hurting anyone else, so what's the problem?
- Everyone else is doing it, so why not me too?

Do any of those sound familiar to you? Does something else come to mind? A lot of us are walking around with chains on our ankles and not knowing it, because we think, *If I just suppress this or shove it underneath the rug, surely it will go away.* I'm sorry to say, but that's false. We cannot run away from our problems. They *will* chase us.

We might think our hidden sins are fun and fine, until they're not. Without knowing it, they pull us away from God and slowly decay our spirits and consciences. Even if we try to convince ourselves it's fine or it didn't happen, you always know something is there. Out of sight, out of mind . . . or is it? I've got some news to tell you, though. Eventually, the little secrets or things we hide in the darkness will always be brought into the light, in some shape or form (Luke 12:2).

Before you freak out and panic about someone finding out what you did, I want you to know this is a good thing! Let's talk about it.

Luke 12:2 says, "There is nothing concealed that will not be disclosed, or hidden that will not be made known." That's a promise, not a threat. Bringing things into the light is how we find freedom. The light is the place where we can walk with a clear conscience. It's where we feel fully known. It's where we can stop digging ourselves into a further grave—and it's where God can heal us. But if we continue to walk in the darkness, the enemy will continue to enslave us. Where there is light, darkness cannot be. The two cannot coexist. Light will always overpower darkness. It's biblical *and* scientific. Do you want freedom? You have the choice to decide if you want to get well and bring it into the light, or stay captured in darkness. Let's take a look at an example of this.

John 5 tells the story of a man who was unable to walk for thirty-eight years. This man was lying near a pool called Bethesda, in hopes that he would be healed by this seemingly magical pool. Jesus took notice of the man when no one else had and asked him one simple question: "Do you want to get well?" (v. 6). Instead of answering the question, he responds with some excuses: "I have no one to help me into the pool when the water is stirred. While I am trying to get in, someone else goes down ahead of me" (v. 7). After this, Jesus immediately healed the man, who got up and walked.

We may not know all the reasons why this man offered excuses, but Jesus had compassion on him and healed him anyway. Maybe the man thought, *This is just how I am, so why keep trying?* Or maybe he was sick and tired of trying and failing. Both plausible reasons. But this story can pertain to us when Jesus asks us the very same question, "Do you want to get well?"

Do you want to stay in shame and secrecy? Or do you want to expose it and find freedom? Thankfully, you don't have to do it alone! The Holy Spirit will help you. He's the reason I've overcome my past addictions. By the Holy Spirit giving me the tools, conviction, grace, and power to overcome my sin, I've been able to walk consistently in freedom and not go back to the very thing that enslaved me. He can do the same for you. We just have to cry out, "God, I need you to help me overcome this. I cannot do this on my own." The Holy Spirit is called a helper for a reason (John 14:26)! Just as Jesus had compassion on this man in the story, he has compassion for you in whatever you are going through.

Another way to find freedom is to share with someone, which I know sounds absolutely terrifying. But the more you share, the less weight your past or struggle holds and the less it has power over you. It's funny because you would think that if you share what's keeping you ashamed, people will hold it over your head and judge you—but in reality, people will usually care more and want to help you. If you are wondering who to share it with, it's got to be the right people. Look for people who are safe, reliable, non-judgmental, and will pray for you and follow up with you.

James 5:16 (emphasis added) says, "Therefore *confess* your sins to each other and *pray* for each other so that you may be healed. The prayer of a righteous person is powerful and effective." It's biblical for us to confess and share what we are going through. This means asking friends for prayer and accountability, allowing them to speak into your situation and to help you. My friends and I do this often. If I'm struggling, I text a friend and tell them where I'm messing up and ask for accountability in it, even if I don't want to tell them. Then my friends, being the kind friends they are, pray for me and ask me again in two weeks how I'm doing. They hold me accountable! I hope yours do too. Refer to chapter 4 for help in this. Confession can come in the form of a regular, safe friend group, a small church group, a parent, or a best friend, but you'll want the same people who care consistently for you.

I know this may seem so scary, but it actually makes you feel lighter and freer. Try it and see what happens. The enemy wants you to keep your mouth shut, because in darkness, he keeps you enslaved. Growing up, my youth pastor told us, "The power of sin is in secrecy." This quote stuck with me because it's so true! Live in the light, expose your darkness, and watch those shackles fall off. Don't give the enemy a foothold in your life with a closed mouth. The enemy must flee in the light.

Often, the person who you don't want to share the most with is the person you usually need to tell first. Use your discernment to choose someone trustworthy. Your heart might begin to race, and you might feel like trembling before and while telling someone, but trust me, once you say it out loud, you'll feel the weight lift off your shoulders. *Ahh, sweet freedom!* You can do this. Say it with me: "I can do this!"

Proverbs 28:13 says, "Whoever conceals their sins does not prosper, but the one who confesses and renounces them finds mercy." In my own story, once I let people in, I could finally get the help I needed. My friends and family lovingly walked alongside me as I healed, dealt with legalities, moved out of my apartment, and finished up my senior year of college. I couldn't have done it without them. I thought they would disown me or leave me in my mess, but instead they picked me up out of my pit. Even though I was afraid my family would be disappointed in me or angry with me, I knew I couldn't keep living the way I'd been living. I was embarrassed and terrified to tell my sister what I'd done, but I felt significantly better once I did. I knew deep down that I needed someone to pull me out of it. Once I opened up, the healing and change began. We don't heal in isolation.

Sharing Your Story

I shared my story to show you that it no longer has power over me—and neither should yours. For years, I was terrified of sharing this story in fear that people would judge, label, and misunderstand me. But what I have come to find is that my story, as messy as it is, has helped others find freedom. The more I share it, the more I see God use it. Even though my story is not something I would have chosen for myself, it's now something I will use to help prevent others from choosing a similar path. Your story can be used for God's glory and may have the key that others need for their freedom too!

I don't know what has happened to you, who has hurt you, or what you've done, but no matter how difficult the details of your story are, you are not identified by it and your future is not determined by it. Thank God! If it's something you've done, God has already forgiven you (1 John 1:9). Nothing you can do will make you exempt from his love. If it's something that has happened to you, my heart aches for you. I know God is going to help you overcome it and heal from it. Your story may not be done being written, but there's beauty in that. There's still time for your story—and you—to be restored. You're not out of time.

What's surprising is you never know who else has a similar story to yours, but if you begin to open up and share it, you'll suddenly see you're not alone. When I shared on my podcast about struggling with masturbation and porn, I had so many women message me and share that they struggled with the same thing. Who knew! They felt so alone and ashamed of this secret sin they were carrying around for so long, but once they heard another woman speak up about it, they suddenly felt seen and heard. So my encouragement to you is, don't keep your story hidden. Share it. Whether you're getting to know someone or spending time with a longtime friend, take time to ask them their story and share yours. I've found over and over that so many people want to be heard and known, but not enough people ask them the questions to get there. You'll be surprised to find what you might have in common! Your vulnerability and bravery might be needed in order to help others feel comfortable to do the same.

However, you may need to get healing before sharing your story. I know I did. Surround yourself with people who can help you privately heal before sharing publicly. Before you call it your testimony, go through the test fully. Share from a healed place, not a hurt place. I waited so long to share my story because I didn't want to come online bitter, angry, and vengeful, but rather share from a place of healing and a desire to help others. This is important because sometimes we share to vent and trauma-bond with others instead of sharing from a testimony of victory and freedom.

When I've met other women who have similar stories to mine, I feel encouraged and seen. Talking with someone who understands my unique pain was healing for me. But other times, my friends and I would ping-pong back and forth between whose ex was worse and whose story was more dramatic; at least, that's what it felt like! We bonded over a shared trauma and continued to perpetuate the problem because it was a commonality between us, but it honestly prolonged healing and prevented us from going deeper in other areas of our lives that had gone untouched. There is so much more to us than just our past and pain! Let's learn from it, but know that it is not our identity.

The enemy would love to use your pain and past to take you down. His main objective is to steal, kill, and destroy. But here comes God, ready to cleanse you and give you life more abundantly (John 10:10). The enemy wants you to stay silent because he knows the ripple effect that your story will have on many others' lives. Boom, got 'em! Not today, Satan!

Biblical Examples

Let's go back to the Bible to meet someone who had a life-changing encounter with Jesus and immediately went to tell others so they also could be free.

In John 4:1–29, Jesus meets a Samaritan woman gathering water at a well outside her village. He asks her for water, but because he was a Jew and she was a Samaritan, she was shocked that Jesus would even talk to her. At this time, Jews did not associate with Samaritans. Jesus went out of his way (per usual) to go to this part of town that he didn't need to in order to meet with this woman. She was at the well to gather water, but Jesus offers her true Living Water—aka himself, the only person who can fully satisfy her needs. She still doesn't quite understand that the Living Water he's referring to is himself, but she desires it, because she doesn't want to keep returning over and over.

Jesus cuts to the chase and tells this woman to go grab her husband, and she responds, "I have no husband" (v. 17). And Jesus responds to her, "You are right when you say you have no husband. The fact is, you have had five husbands, and the man you now have is not your husband. What you have just said is quite true" (John 4:17–18). *Mic drop, Jesus!* Jesus truthfully yet gracefully calls this woman out on her past and current lifestyle. She has had five husbands and is now sleeping with a man who is not even her husband. But Jesus doesn't shame her; he offers her living water for her soul. Being overfilled with love and joy, she leaves her jar at the well and runs into town to tell everyone she met the Messiah.

This story is powerful for many reasons! It shows us that even though you may have a bad reputation or painful history, God will go out of his way to notice you and rescue you. Even though I'm sure this woman was ashamed of her past, God uses her to tell others the good news of Jesus. Her story did not discredit her of being worthy of Jesus's presence and being the carrier of good news. Notice that she leaves her jar at the well and runs into the town. This jar could resemble her no longer needing a physical jar for water because Jesus had given her spiritual water that set her free. Once you're set free by Jesus, you leave the past behind and run to tell others what Jesus did for you! "So if the Son sets you free, you will be free indeed" (John 8:36)!

No matter your story, don't let people shame you for it. It's called your past for a reason. Leave it in the past, just like God has. You're a new creation in Christ now. If you've had several divorces like this woman or an annulment like me, or something else, you're not disqualified. We are all broken people in need of a Savior.

When you take those broken pieces to Jesus, watch what he can do. He has transformed many people's messes into ministries. I've seen that in my own life. That doesn't mean you have to write a book or start a YouTube channel (though you might!). A friend of mine who was highly addicted to drugs in college and later healed by God now helps homeless men recover from drug addictions. I know a couple who got divorced and then, by the grace of God, they restored their relationship and got remarried! Now they counsel other couples in marriage restoration. The power of God's redemption! You never know how God wants to use your story and for whom—whether that's helping with your church's youth group, volunteering at a pregnancy crisis center, or being willing to sit down and pray with someone who is struggling with the same sin that once held you captive.

What If I Don't Have a So-Called Testimony?

Last, I want to talk to the people who might think, *I don't have a wild past or dramatic testimony. Where do I belong?* I've had many people ask me this, and I just want to say to you, you are blessed. It shows God's protection over your life and your obedience to him. Having what you may think of as no testimony is a testimony in itself. Praise God that you don't have scars, trauma, or difficult regrets. You didn't have to go through difficult things to perhaps learn the same lessons as others. It doesn't discount you at all from sharing your story. Instead, share how God does move in your life and how God's Word offers a more enriched life by following it!

I pray you now know the power of confession and of sharing your testimony. I hope you're encouraged to boldly and courageously share your story, to point people toward our Savior who sets us free. If that's over lunch, on social media, to a random person you meet, or even in a book, you can help someone else know Jesus and become free too. I pray too that my story helps someone else reading this know that you are not alone, and you can find freedom and healing one day from the very thing you thought would enslave you forever. Happy and healthy people are free people!

MAKE IT REAL IN YOUR LIFE

1. What is something you're holding on to that you need freedom from?
2. Who is someone you believe you could confess to?
3. What is something that you can praise God for helping you overcome?
4. What is something from your testimony that God can use to help others?
5. How can you use your story to give God glory?

11

Set Apart

How to Be Okay Being Different

It was a warm, sunny day in Portugal in the summer of 2021. I was a little jet-lagged but excited to spend two weeks in a beautiful new country with my best friend Penny. Once I arrived at my accommodation, I ran to open the window, and I saw the ocean in the distance. *Ahh . . . fresh, salty air.* I closed my eyes and took a deep breath as the sun beamed on my skin. I ran over to the next window and saw some campers arriving with their luggage and surfboards. People from all around the world had traveled to this surf camp to experience new cultures, meet new people, and surf for a whole week. I had been hired by the company to promote their camps online to my followers—and also to hopefully improve my surfing, of course! I was beyond stoked and grateful to be there.

Shortly into the trip, I realized people weren't there only to surf. Each night, after surfing all day, people would get dressed up to party and drink. I don't want to judge because that was once me, but since faithfully walking with God, my life has looked quite different. Instead of going, my friend and I would read and chat together in our room and head to sleep early to be refreshed for the morning surf session.

During the mornings, I would sit in the sun on the patio to spend time in the Word. Some of the campers I had met would come up to me and ask, "Are you reading the Bible?" One guy from Germany actually said to me, "I've never even opened a Bible." My heart began to race and my palms started to sweat, because all I wanted to do was share my faith and not be weird about it. But I felt this pressure because I thought, *What if this is the only time he gets to hear about God?* I gathered myself and asked him questions about his faith and upbringing, and he shared with me that he didn't like church and thought it was quite boring. *Hey bud, I get it.* I felt the same growing up. But the more I talked to him, the more I realized he had never encountered the real presence of God. That's what changes people and sets them free. I prayed underneath my breath that God would speak through me and let me be a light to him. I'm not sure where this man is now, but I know that faith seeds were planted, and I am trusting the Lord to water them however and whenever he will.

As the camp continued, the partying did as well. On the last night of the camp, there was a full-on party with a DJ, drinks, snacks, and decor, and everyone wore white. My friend and I went for a bit to chat and dance with people, but people kept asking us why we weren't drinking. It's not that I wasn't tempted, but I just knew that I didn't want to go back to my old ways. But this gave me the chance to share more of my faith and values as people kept asking, and they sure thought we were weird.

You don't have sex and get drunk? they all asked. One girl in particular approached me to ask how I was like this. How was I able to not participate? Why didn't I care what they thought? I pulled her aside to help her feel more comfortable, and she began to share with me that she didn't want to party either but constantly felt pressured by her friends. She opened up to me about her struggle with masturbation and porn and how she'd tried so hard to quit but couldn't. I got to share with her my faith and how I was able to overcome that same struggle through Jesus. I was a bit nervous doing this. I was afraid I would say the wrong thing and scare her off, but eventually I prayed over her and led her to know Jesus. We hugged with tears in our eyes, and she thanked me. It was such an amazing, memorable night that I still praise God for, and she and I still communicate to this day.

Being different, set apart, may be difficult, but it's worth it when it has the power to change someone else's life. What does it mean to be set apart? I'll give you all my tips on being okay with being different from everyone else (in a good way) and standing firm in your convictions, even when it's challenging. I know this may seem tough, but don't worry, I'm here to help!

Be Different

Being set apart isn't my idea. I actually want to fit in most of the time. I spent most of my life trying to fit in, and we saw where that got me—a lot of unwise decisions, lack of identity, lack of confidence, and not understanding who God called me to be. I think deep down, everyone wants to be accepted and seen as cool. I know being different isn't usually seen as being cool—unless you are the trendsetter in town—but typically, we all just want to fit in. But being set apart is about saying no to the things you know are wrong or that go against your convictions, and instead going the other way. I know this is easier said than done, but with the help of the Holy Spirit, time, and good people around you, it's possible. I'm going to show you how.

> Do not be conformed to this world, but be transformed by the renewal of your mind, that by testing you may discern what is the will of God, what is good and acceptable and perfect.
> For by the grace given to me I say to everyone among you not to think of himself more highly than he ought to think, but to think with sober judgment, each according to the measure of faith that God has assigned.
>
> Romans 12:2–3 ESV

In other words, do not look like the world. Be set apart. What does the Bible mean when it refers to the *world*? It means people who don't know Jesus and are living a life contrary to his Word. On the other hand, Christians are referred to as "aliens" (1 Peter 2:11 NABRE). Funny, I know, but it doesn't literally mean those green, bug-eyed, alien-looking things. It means that for Christians, earth is not our home. Keep tracking with me! This isn't some conspiracy theory I'm trying to convince you to believe, I promise. But once you become a follower of Christ, your real citizenship is in heaven (Philippians 3:20). Earth is a holding place until we spend eternity with Jesus in heaven. Since this isn't our home, we shouldn't get too comfortable. Our time here is limited, so we should use it wisely and help others become citizens of heaven too. Being set apart is a mark of a Christian because we will not be able to effectively share our faith and deeply follow Jesus if we continue to look like everyone else and are constantly entertaining the world's false promises.

Being set apart is doing what others may not do. For example, when everyone else goes to the bars to get blackout drunk, you stay home with your dog and make yourself a nice dinner. Or when all your friends are watching a movie with a lot of nudity, you look away or leave. Or you hang out with the girl everyone else deems weird or non-important. To be honest, being set apart can be lonely at times. It will require shedding some people and environments that no longer better you and shape you into the person God has called you to be—the person you know you can be. It might shake your friendships or cause people to think you are being a prude, when in reality you are just trying to follow Jesus, because you know his ways bring a more fulfilled life (John 10:10). When people see your life and how being set apart brings you more joy and freedom, they may begin to understand and want the same thing. But it starts with you and God.

It may require you looking dumb, or people calling you names, or people saying, "You've changed," and with that, you can gently respond, "I have, and I'm happy I have." I know looking different is scary, and you might feel like I did—wanting only to fit in and be liked. But fitting in and being liked shouldn't come with a cost. I would rather you feel a little lonelier or be misunderstood than conform to society's ways that are nothing but fool's gold. Sin and the world will always overpromise and never deliver. They will say, "You only live once! Do whatever you want!" But that can leave you feeling empty and shameful. Once I stepped away from the places and people that kept hurting me and chose God for myself, the freedom and healing began. I did lose friends along the way, and you might too. But wait and see how God will replace friendships and better you.

Your lonely nights of saying no to the party or to that boy you know isn't good for you will be rewarded by God, who sees your actions when you could have caved (Matthew 6:6–7). The no's will be worth it when they lead to a yes from God later on as he sees your purity, intentions, and heart in private. We prepare for the public moments in the private moments. In the private, quiet times with God is where you gear up for battle out in public. Studying God's Word to know who he calls you to be and what he's calling you out of is so important. God calls you so much higher because he knows you are made for more. Leaving people and things behind that pull you away from God for the sake of godliness will always be rewarded by God.

> Do not love the world or the things in the world. If anyone loves the world, the love of the Father is not in him. For all that is in the world—the desires of the flesh and the desires of the eyes and pride of life—is not from the Father but is from the world. And the world is passing away along with its desires, but whoever does the will of God abides forever.
>
> 1 John 2:15–17 ESV

We may not see the rewards now, but the reward is knowing that God will honor your obedience and sacrifice. His approval is all that matters. He wants to protect us from the harmful temptations of this world out of his love for you. God doesn't ask us to be different just for the sake of being different, but because it produces fruit, godliness, and effectiveness in sharing our faith.

Don't Do It Alone

Being set apart is a lot easier when you have the right people around you. When you walk with other Christ followers through this life, suddenly you don't feel alone anymore. You feel less strange because the people around you also want to look different. They'll help you make wise decisions when you feel you can't on your own—and you'll do the same for them. We need each other. Together, your desires to follow Jesus and help others do the same will feel encouraged and championed. When I reflect on my past, in all the times I changed my life and unhealthy patterns, people were always a part of it.

People are essential for positive and consistent change. On that trip to Portugal, having my friend Penny with me helped both of us stick to our values and remain faithful to God's Word. We were both committed to the same thing. If you feel like you are struggling and slipping back into your old ways, invite someone in to help you not run back to old habits and struggles. Two are better than one. Finding godly friends will take time, but please don't stop praying for them. God doesn't want you to be alone either, despite how alone you may feel right now. This is just for a season, and it will pass! Here are three categories to help you live a set-apart life.

Be set apart with your words

Our words matter. They represent our beliefs, morals, prejudices, and principles—sometimes in ways we may not mean. And our words have the power to build up or destroy. There will be times when people around you are negative, fearful, gossipy, unkind, or dishonest, and this is your chance to be the opposite. Aim to be positive, hopeful, encouraging, complimentary, and truthful, providing a biblical perspective even when others aren't. People will notice your words and eventually be thankful for them. Here are some examples:

> When a group of girls is gossiping about someone not at the table, you can kindly tell them it's inappropriate and that you choose to believe the best of the person not present.
>
> When others are fearful about the economy crashing, you can talk about how you know God is our provider and helper in times of need.
>
> When someone is complaining about everything and bringing down the mood, try not to join in. Misery loves company. Instead, empathize with them and encourage them.

One time at the gym, my trainer said in front of the whole group, "I've never heard Jeanine cuss once." This felt like the biggest compliment to me because I used to cuss a lot in my past, and I made a conscious effort to change that since growing my relationship with Jesus. Being set apart isn't always the biggest, flashiest things but sometimes the small, consistent differences that people take notice of and wonder why you are different, and then you can point them back to your faith as to why that is. Your words have power!

Be set apart with your standards

Your convictions, opinions, beliefs, attitudes, and standards will stick out to others when they look contrary to popular belief, which may cause some ruffling of feathers. This isn't the time to be haughty or boastful about your beliefs and opinions but rather an opportunity to live them out. Your life is more of a sermon than your mouth ever will be. You cannot expect people to want to follow Jesus if they don't even see him in you. By simply living the way you do, people will see much more clearly how Jesus's ways are better than if we tried to argue our point instead. Our standards should be based on the Word of God—a constant and consistent truth we can always go back to when society's standards change.

These standards could look like working an entire eight-hour shift even if the boss is gone or your coworker leaves early and still takes credit for a full shift. Or this could look like you and your partner choosing to wait to have sex until marriage and trusting God's design for intimacy, even when others around you aren't. Or when you believe there is an injustice somewhere, you fight for truth and justice, even when people don't.

Your standards and values may upset people. People don't often like it when someone goes against the grain or challenges their beliefs. In the polarizing world that we live in today, standing firm on God's Word is increasingly difficult. "Be on your guard; stand firm in the faith; be courageous; be strong" (1 Corinthians 16:13). Keep going, knowing that if your convictions are godly and biblical, you only need to please God, not others. Jesus calls people blessed when they are persecuted for his name's sake (Matthew 5:10–12). So consider yourself blessed!

Here's a verse I remind myself of when I am tempted to live for people's approval instead of God's. "Am I now trying to win the approval of human beings, or of God? Or am I trying to please people? If I were still trying to please people, I would not be a servant of Christ" (Galatians 1:10).

Be set apart with your actions

The old saying "Actions speak louder than words" applies here too! Sometimes our consistent actions that others may see as abnormal may still be respected. In whatever you do, do it with love and for the glory of God. Don't take your differences and standing out as something to be prideful of, but rather a way to serve God with a humble heart.

Being set apart can look like blessing people and helping others even when no one else is. For example, offering to people, "Hey, can

152

I get you water? Can I take your plate? Do you need a ride? Do you need help moving?" Having a servant's heart really helps people notice something different about you. Doing helpful things with pure motives and humility will help unbelievers notice and wonder, "Why are you doing that? You don't have to take my dishes, you don't have to buy my coffee, you don't have to help me when I know you're busy." It lets them see Jesus in you without even having to utter the word *Jesus*. It's going out of your way to make someone feel loved and seen.

After watching you consistently be different over time, someone may ask you, "I've noticed you're always so joyful and helpful. Why is that?" And there is your door to share your faith or be an example of God's love to someone who may need it.

People are out there struggling, and they need your light and the hope of Jesus. But take a breath and know that it's not solely up to you. When you partner with God's Holy Spirt, he will give you the words to speak and help you make wise decisions. Matthew 10:19 (NASB) says, "But when they hand you over, do not worry about how or what you are to say; for what you are to say will be given you in that hour." Pray that God would help you to speak and act the way he calls you to in a moment of need. You don't have to do this alone.

Maybe you feel unable to be set apart right now to help others because you're not fully there yet yourself—I understand, that was me for a while. Change and transformation is a process. Overcoming sin and temptations is a lot easier with grace upon yourself, people around you, and knowing that there is nothing you cannot overcome with God.

> No temptation has overtaken you that is not common to man. God is faithful, and he will not let you be tempted beyond your ability, but with the temptation he will also provide the way of escape, that you may be able to endure it.
>
> 1 Corinthians 10:13 ESV

God will always provide a way out for you. He will always help you overcome. But you must feed your spirit (through prayer, godly music, the Word, people) to help you follow him closely and make godly decisions. Out of the overflow of alone moments with God, you will be able to fight off what holds you back.

I pray as I close this chapter that you see how being different is okay. You weren't meant to just conform and fit in. Being different is not something to be ashamed of but embraced, because in a culture that pushes conformity in beliefs and values, yours may be the very reason someone else finds God one day too. Don't let the world's ways prevent you from becoming happy and healthy. Fulfilling God's calling on your life will always have you go against the grain and choose a narrower road, but the reward in the end is always worth the risk. God blesses those who choose holiness over comfort. Let's be people set apart for his glory!

MAKE IT REAL IN YOUR LIFE

1. What areas are you not being set apart in?
2. What are some convictions or actions in your life that people may not agree with?
3. How can you be different in your own environments?
4. What do you feel still holds you back from being different?
5. When was a time you overcame a temptation to conform?

---— 12 ---—

Wellness

How to Take Care of Yourself from the Inside Out

When I moved to LA, I was starry-eyed with excitement. I saw the mountains in the distance, felt the perfect weather every day, and was excited to be in a new city in an attempt to accomplish my dreams. I was excited to leave Dallas and try something new because all I had ever known was Texas.

Los Angeles was very different from my hometown. From the people to the food, weather, activities, fashion, and lifestyle, it couldn't be more different. People loved to dress up every day in their newest outfit, work out in the trendiest classes, and do anything and everything to look and feel good. Look, I'm not trying to judge anyone, because I quickly noticed I was doing the same. Within the first year of living there, I embarked on what I thought of as my new self-improvement journey. I cut dairy and gluten from my diet (because everyone was telling me to), dyed my hair, got lash extensions, joined the trendy gym, and did whatever it took to fit in. I became obsessed with self-care, to the point of it consuming my every thought from the second I woke up.

Now, while I don't think there is anything wrong with self-care, it can quickly become self-obsession and even an idol. An idol is anything we value more than God. We begin to worship ourselves and our bodies and remove anyone or anything that no longer serves us. While I think there are benefits to weeding out the bad, this practice can quickly turn into doing only things that are self-seeking. We think all we need is ourselves and no one else. We become so inwardly focused, constantly trying to look and feel good, that we stop looking outward and noticing what others may need. I love self-growth and think it is essential, but I have noticed in my own life that it can easily become an addiction. Soon after settling into LA, my entire focus was on bettering myself. It wasn't until I sought out a counselor and nutritionist that I realized my obsession had gone too far. I was draining myself trying to always look good, and it came from an unhealthy place inside me that I wasn't able to identify at the time.

Digging into the *why* behind what we are doing is so important. What is your intention or your motivation? If we look at my story, I was doing things from a place of hating my body, trying to fit in, and keeping up with people rather than a place of genuinely trying to be healthy, working out because I loved it, and not just doing things for my present self but also for my future self. Perhaps you feel this way too. You want to better yourself, which is maybe why you picked up this book, but you don't know how to get there or your methods aren't working. What I've learned is that in pursuing a long, healthy life, bringing people and God into the process helps keep our motives and intentions pure. Sometimes our desires aren't wrong, but the *why* behind them is. I wanted to be healthy, but the methods I took to get there weren't.

Part of becoming happy and healthy is taking care of ourselves from the inside out—mind, body, soul. The more we take care of the internal, the more it positively affects the external.

These three elements are like gauges to our body. If one is off, our body will start telling us. If we don't take care of it, it might start affecting the other elements. Our body is always trying to speak to us, whether in the form of our stomach bloating from eating improper food, getting a headache from overconsumption of light from our phones, or feeling anxious because something is bothering you that is going unaddressed. Here's a fun fact: God wants us to take care of ourselves. He says in 1 Corinthians 6:19–20 that our bodies are a temple, which means that our bodies are to be treated with care like a holy place. In the Old Testament, a temple was a sacred meeting place for the Israelites. So if God compares our bodies to a holy temple, it must mean that he wants us to treat them as such.

I believe God wants us to take care of our bodies in a healthy way and honor him in the process, with pure intentions. My hope for you in this chapter is that you leave with new ways to steward your health by taking care of yourself from the inside out. I wish I did it sooner! Doing so will produce a holistic, fruitful, and healthy life. Ready to begin?

Mind

Our mind is extremely powerful. It tells our bodies what to do and how to do it. According to Dr. Caroline Leaf, a cognitive neuroscientist specializing in cognitive and metacognitive neuropsychology, "Where your mind goes, your brain simply follows. So if you train your mind to be in order, your brain will actually follow the process."[1] Our mind is in charge of our thought life, how we process information, what we believe about ourselves, how we make decisions, and a long list of many other things.

What we think about consistently is who we will become. For centuries, God's Word has provided the same wisdom science now offers. Proverbs 23:7 (NKJV) says, "For as he thinks in his heart, so is he." Therefore, your thoughts and mind have a lot of power to determine your actions and beliefs. If this is the case, then we must be mindful of what flows in and out of our minds. That can be what we watch, read, listen to, think about, and even who speaks into us. What we input is what we will output. If we want to output beneficial, encouraging, holy, godly things, then we must input things that contribute to that. This will require some shedding on your part of things that aren't helping you grow. Maybe you love watching crime shows or horror movies, but if you find yourself having nightmares a lot, or feeling constantly paranoid, or fearing the dark, it might be time to say good-bye to the shows. We can't grow from the things that hurt us.

Or maybe you feel constantly anxious. It's important to audit the source of your anxiety. Maybe you constantly live in fear, worry, and doubt of the future or about finances, or about being single forever. The Bible says in Isaiah 26:3 (emphasis added), "You will keep in perfect peace those whose *minds* are steadfast, because they trust in you." Our minds are emphasized here because most things start with our minds. I'm not going to downplay that some people severely struggle with anxiety or mental health, but I am always going to encourage you to try to identify the root of your issues. A mind that is steadfast and unwavering from God's Word is a more peaceful mind. If you are still struggling, that's okay too. Consider bringing someone into it and having them help you process through your worries and doubts and pray over you.

The results of a 2020 study reported people may have more than six thousand thoughts per day.[2] That's a lot! I would definitely consider myself an overthinker, which probably means I have about ten thousand thoughts per day. Well, maybe. I'm not sure! But I know a lot of my thoughts are pretty weird or random, like *Do fish ever get thirsty?* or *Who let the dogs out?*

But others are heavier, like *I feel like no one cares about me* or *Am I even making an impact in my job?* Some heavy thoughts turn destructive, filling your mind with lies if you're not careful, and eventually they can gain enough power to rule over you. These negative thoughts and thought patterns will cause us to live and walk out that lie in other areas of our lives. It can quickly become a downward spiral. For me, if I don't catch negative thoughts like these, they can easily cause me to pull away from people, want to run and hide, and totally self-destruct. All it takes is one whispered lie from the enemy to send me into a downward spiral.

Second Corinthians 10:5 says, "We demolish arguments and every pretension [claim] that sets itself up against the knowledge of God, and we take captive every thought to make it obedient to Christ." The second part denotes that the arguments and claims start with our thoughts. In order to keep our minds healthy, we must capture thoughts and make them obedient to what God says about us. In other words, we must replace the lies with God's truth. If we don't catch those little lies, they settle into our thoughts and grow into something worse than we ever imagined. A thought becomes a mindset, a mindset becomes a habit, a habit becomes a lifestyle, a lifestyle becomes an identity. So be mindful! If you want to start your day off on the right foot, start with the right mindset. Your mindset will determine the direction of your life.

When we have our minds fixed on positive, encouraging things, our brains and bodies can follow, just as Dr. Leaf stated. What are other ways we can keep our minds sharp and healthy? Here are some of my ideas!

Books

First, you know by now that I will always encourage you to read and know the Word of God! It is powerful and effective to change your life. On top of that, many self-help books are super beneficial! If you're really struggling with something and you need a new way of thinking, try to find a book that speaks specifically to that issue. If you don't like to read, try audiobooks. So many amazing books are out there, covering a vast number of topics to help keep your mind sharp.

Podcasts

As a podcast host myself, I love podcasts! If reading isn't your thing, try listening to podcasts—specifically, shows that break down the Bible for you, help you in your business, or give you motivation for things you are working through. You are always welcome to join me on my podcast, *Happy and Healthy*, every Tuesday, where we dive deeper into these types of conversations. With the vast number of podcasts available today, you can be sure to find one that will help you in almost any area you are looking for. If you want to listen to the Bible daily, *The Bible Recap* is great for that. If you want help in your personal finances, check out Dave Ramsey's *The Ramsey Show*. Or if you want a conversation on navigating adulting, the *Becoming Something* podcast is amazing.

Counseling

While counseling may not fix everything, it's a good start. If there is something you are struggling with mentally, look into counseling. Having someone to listen to you and process things with can be both cathartic and resolving. I've done it many times before and found it to be extremely beneficial. There is no shame in seeking out professional help. If you are a Christian like me, I recommend seeking out a Christian counselor who can give you biblical advice too. Remember that a good counselor is supposed to help you process situations and find healing but not to have you be dependent on them forever.

Learn new things

Engage regularly in activities that stimulate and challenge your brain. Constantly pushing and challenging our brains is going to keep us sharper by using parts of our brains that may decline if we only scroll on social media for hours. Consider learning a language or a new sport, doing puzzles, playing games like chess or Scrabble, solving numerical problems, studying difficult topics, and challenging your dexterity, spatial reasoning, and logic. Each of these activities can help you stay mentally healthy and challenge your brain.

Music

Music plays a massive role in our lives. You might pay attention to what you put into your body when it comes to food, but how often do you pay attention to the music entering your mind? Music has the power to instantly change our moods by hyping us up, making us feel sad, or soothing us in a stressful time. However, music that only talks about sex, anxiety, or heartbreak will eventually wear on you mentally. Studies show that music can impact our mood long-term, increasing depression or anxiety. You may not see the effects, but just because you don't see it, doesn't mean it's not happening. Consider worship music or podcasts instead that encourage and uplift your spirit, rather than diminish it.

All of these are great ways to grow and challenge our minds, and they offer a strategy for putting something beneficial into our minds rather than filling up on fluff or damaging words or images that may lead to lies or decay. Our brains are extremely malleable, meaning we can influence our brain development in positive or negative directions. The more we engage and challenge our mind and body, the longer our brains function at a high level. Once you consistently fill your mind with encouraging, godly things, abundant life and truth will begin to naturally flow out of you.

Body

As I talked about in the opening of this chapter, I had to seek out help from a nutritionist. I was struggling with yo-yo dieting, constantly feeling bloated and tired, struggling with acne and low self-esteem, and not knowing what to eat in order to aid my body. What's funny, though, is I sought counsel from her to help me become skinnier, but she actually helped me overcome a borderline disorder. With her help, I finally was able to see food and my body differently. I learned that neither food nor my body were the enemy; the lies feeding my insecurity and obsessive habits were. Working with a nutritionist taught me what foods were more nutritious for me to consume, how to stop obsessing over numbers on a scale, how to listen to my body, and how to see my body as a good and powerful tool I could use to work for me, not against me.

Do you relate to my story at all? Feeling constantly down about your body or feeling slow or just bleh? Hopefully this section can encourage you to make some positive changes. We only get one body, and I want you to make the most of it! I'm no doctor, but here are some ways I take care of my body.

Working out

Naturally in the body section, I will start with physical activity. Science proves that working out or engaging in some sort of physical activity leads to many benefits, such as better sleep and mood, increased brain health, stress reduction, lessened symptoms of depression and anxiety, a lower risk for some diseases, and so much more. And not only that, it increases your chances of living longer. Seems like a no-brainer! However, I know getting going can be challenging. Refer back to chapter 7 for some tips on how to start building this habit.

Working out is not one-size-fits-all, so you will have to find something that works for you. Maybe that is taking a daily walk, boxing, getting a trainer, following an online program, dancing, or joining a sports league. Whatever you choose, see it as something you *get* to do, not *have* to do.

Getting your heart rate up and moving your body consistently is something you may not want to do, but you can always try to pair it with something you already enjoy, like watching a TV show while you walk on the treadmill, or starting super small—like parking at the back of a parking lot so you walk farther to get to the store. Or if you're competitive, sign up for a race or contest a few months down the road and begin prepping for it in advance. To be consistent, plan your week out and add it to your daily calendar.

This could be a fifteen-minute walk as you start out. Something is better than nothing.

If you want to reach a certain goal, though, or achieve a certain physique, you may need to get on a program or reach out to a professional. No matter where you're starting or what your physical goals are, your body is an amazing thing—right now, exactly how it is today. After all, it's what gets you from point A to point B, gets you out of bed, digests food for you, and so much more. Be thankful for what it can do for you right now. It took me a good bit to figure out my workout routine, but once I did, I was so much more joyful, energized, and mentally positive throughout my day. It has genuinely improved my life overall and will for yours too!

Drinking water

In order for our bodies to function properly, they need water daily. Drinking "about 15.5 cups (3.7 liters) of fluids a day for men" and "about 11.5 cups (2.7 liters) of fluids a day for women" can aid in reducing brain fog, bloating, skin issues, and body toxins, as well as improving important bodily functions.[3] Try carrying a water bottle with you everywhere you go and leaving a cup of water by your bed so you can drink it before you go to sleep and right when you wake up. Find what works for you and try to hit those water goals!

Eating healthy

Food to our bodies is like fuel to a car. If we want it to run properly, we need to give it the proper nutrients, and only the right kinds of foods can sustain us throughout the day. I'm not saying to cut out Chick-fil-A from your life completely (that would be a crime), but have fast food in moderation. If you are noticing a ton of symptoms like low energy, acne, bloating, poor concentration, severe weight gain, etc., it might be time to check what you're eating or get tested for allergies. I changed what I ate a little over three years ago and noticed a significant improvement in my gut health, mood, and overall feeling in my body.

Try incorporating more protein, fiber, fruits and vegetables, whole grain foods, and nutrient-rich foods like salmon, kale, blueberries, or eggs into meals. Also, cooking from home more often than eating out can reduce consumption of excess carbohydrates, sodium, sugars, fats, and sneaky unhealthy ingredients. If you are limited on time, try to meal prep once a week. It will help set yourself up for success throughout the week!

Moderation and substitutions are key. If you genuinely love chocolate or candy (like I do), you don't have to remove them completely or forever. Instead, have a small amount once a week instead of eating them every day or a whole bag in one sitting. I also like to find healthier alternatives, like dark chocolate instead of a more processed Snickers bar. There are many ways to still enjoy the things you love with healthier options.

Remember, try to think about doing this not only for yourself but for your future self too. When you are in your forties or fifties, your future self will thank your present self!

Sleep

Sleep is essential. We will die without it, not to be dramatic. Even without that extreme example, sleep affects us deeply. I'm a cranky mess the next day if I don't get enough sleep. It's recommended by the CDC for adults to have at least seven hours of sleep per night, which I know is not always realistic depending on the season, but it's worth trying to make a priority.

Some tips on getting a good night's rest: put your phone across the room, avoid any blue lights from your electronic devices before bed, sleep in a dark room, avoid caffeine after lunch, find the right temperature in your room, and have a comfy mattress and pillow. Bonus tip is spraying some lavender spray on your pillows and getting a sound machine for your room. Works wonders for me!

If you are struggling to fall asleep, consider taking melatonin, drinking tea before bed, praying over yourself, reading a book, or if you have a lot on your mind, try writing your thoughts down and transferring them elsewhere before catching those z's.

Rest

Last, I want to talk about rest, because no matter what you do in this list, you'll struggle to do it well without being rested. I'm not talking about sleep, but more the art of doing nothing or doing something that is actually restorative. Resting is essential for our bodies to recover, rejuvenate, and restore themselves. God himself rested on the seventh day after creating the world, as we read in Exodus 20:8–11, because he wanted to show us that we should too. Hustling and working hard has its time and place, but it's important to make rest a part of your routine. Take a day off at least once a week where you do nothing but be still, sit, lounge, and let your body rest. For me, this looks like cooking a meal at home, getting off my phone a bit, putting my sweatpants on, and watching a movie. As we work on building good routines and habits, make rest a part of that. We work *from* rest, not work *to* rest. Healthy people are rested people.

Soul

Your soul is your inner self. It's the thing that God created inside you to be the identity that makes you who you are. It is the seat of your memory, feelings, imagination, convictions, desires, and affections. Your soul cannot be destroyed either. If you have accepted Jesus as your Savior, it will last forever in heaven with him. Therefore, it's incredibly important.

I also like to think that your soul is what makes you come alive. It's what responds to the things that bring you joy, immense exhilaration, and peace. When I am surfing or snowboarding with my friends, it's those moments that make me go, *Wow, I feel so alive!* I want to do more of that. Similarly, after I get to meet and chat with women who listen to my podcast or follow me on social media and see how God is moving through my platforms to help them, I feel overwhelmed with gratitude and purpose. I think we should do more things that feed our soul and make us feel more alive. Life is too short not to say yes to more things that give us life! Here are some ways to feed your soul and bring more joy.

Do things that bring you life

Think of a time when you felt so happy and overwhelmed by God's goodness. Can you channel that again or—even better—re-create that situation? Was it maybe after you hiked somewhere and got to the top of the mountain and saw the view? Or after you helped serve your community and saw the joy on people's faces? Or maybe it was by hosting a game night at your house and seeing people laugh together and enjoy each other's company. Whatever it was, do that more often! As long as the things are God-honoring and good, do them!

Pray

A soul at peace is a soul that trusts in the Lord, and that comes from a lot of prayer. Prayer edifies our spirit and encourages it. Prayer is what can get us out of the deepest slumps and the roughest spots in our lives. It's what connects us more to the Father, the true source of hope for our souls. If your soul feels tired, try praying this verse:

> Come to me, all you who are weary and burdened, and I will give you rest. Take my yoke upon you and learn from me, for I am gentle and humble in heart, and you will find rest for your souls. For my yoke is easy and my burden is light.
>
> Matthew 11:28–30

He will give you rest for your soul. I pray you feel that today.

Spend time with refreshing people

Something that genuinely always makes my soul feel happy is being around good people who are godly, safe, and fun. These are people who make me laugh, encourage me, and don't take life too seriously. If you have a group of people who are like this in your life, hold on to them and be thankful. Go on a road trip, host a game night, grab dinner together, go to concerts, have deep conversations, and do life consistently with people who are refreshing and make you better.

Express gratitude

A soul full of gratitude consistently is happier and more satisfied. Researchers studied three groups of people for ten weeks. One group was told to write things they were thankful for, another group was told to write things that irritated them, and the third group was told to just write things that happened, without focusing on the good or the bad. Afterward, "those who wrote about gratitude were more optimistic and felt better about their lives. Surprisingly, they also exercised more and had fewer visits to physicians than those who focused on sources of aggravation."[4] This practice can be as simple as writing in your journal or even the Notes app on your phone to record things you are thankful for, or just audibly praying them out loud and thanking God for the blessings in your life.

The Bible says, "Rejoice always, pray continually, give thanks in all circumstances; for this is God's will for you in Christ Jesus" (1 Thessalonians 5:16–18). Even though life will have its inevitable challenges, rejoice, pray, and give thanks to God through the storms. Gratitude is one of the most powerful tools to improve your mood, mind, and mental health. And it's free and simple but often underutilized.

I hope these practical steps help you begin a journey toward health for your mind, body, and soul. By living a more intentional life with a good routine and trying to keep these three elements in balance,

I've seen my joy and mood improve significantly—and I believe it can be the same for you! Now, as I've said throughout this book, you are not expected to do all of these perfectly all the time, but small daily decisions matter. Happiness and health are on the way!

MAKE IT REAL IN YOUR LIFE

1. What are some negative mindsets you have?
2. Is there something in your life that you need to cut out because it is negatively impacting your mind?
3. What is something small you can start doing daily to fuel your body?
4. What are some things that make your soul feel peaceful and alive?
5. Write down three takeaways from this chapter that might help you become healthier.

13

Adventure
How to Embrace New Experiences

The summer before my last semester of college, I got a call from my friend Penny. "Hey, Jeanine, I have a really cool idea I'd love to run by you. . . ." Penny and I were decent friends in college, but we weren't super close at this time. I was a little nervous because I'd known her to be a pretty bold, out-of-the-box person, in the best way possible. I responded, "Sure, what's up?" She told me all about this journey she was starting where she would travel to each state in America and shadow someone's career there. Sounds cool, right? I sure thought it was! In order to kick off her new adventure, she decided she would go to Hawaii first and needed someone to go with her—and she thought of me. Wow, I was honored! I asked her, "Where would we stay?" And, well . . . Penny had a plan that was a bit unusual. "I found this website called Couchsurfers.com, and we can just crash on someone's couch there for the week! It will save us money, and we can be with a local." *Stay on some random person's couch? This girl has lost her mind!* I thought to myself. I hesitantly responded, "Well that's not my first option . . . but if we are trying to ball on a budget, I'll do it!" I found and booked the cheapest flights available. Naturally, I was hesitant at first, but the trip sounded fun, and I'd never been to Hawaii before!

When the time arrived to leave, Penny and I hopped on a flight that would cross the Pacific Ocean and arrive on the beautiful island of Kauai. Right as we landed, we found out that the person we were supposed to stay with had canceled on us. In a panic, we looked at each other and thought *now what?* It was late, and we had nowhere to go and no plan. We immediately called as many hotels as possible, and over and over, we were told they were already booked or were above our budget. I started to really get nervous. I'd never just shown up somewhere without a plan before, but this wasn't anything new for Penny. She was well experienced in this and told me to trust her.

Eventually, we found a quaint little hotel right by the beach. We booked it and set off on our journey. Some of the most amazing and unexpected things happened that week. The first hotel gave us free breakfast and a discount for absolutely no reason. Penny and I be-friended some locals who took us around the whole island, showing us the best, most hidden places. Another resort offered to give us a penthouse suite due to my social media following, where we got the most beautiful view and room. It was unreal! From surfing and bon-fires to cliff jumping, eating sushi, and meeting the locals' families, it was the most amazing trip I had ever been on. Penny and I had the best conversations the whole week, and it really created a true, deep friend-ship. We became close friends and began to do everything together.

Shortly after this trip, she moved to California. She begged me to move there too, and after a year of considering it, I made the leap. Yay! If it weren't for her willingness to be bold and ask me to go to Hawaii, I probably never would have moved to LA and had my life changed there. You never know what saying *yes* may lead to!

The Power of a Yes

I open with this unexpected story to show you that even though you may not know where you are going or what you are doing, a *yes* to something may lead to a *yes* somewhere else—perhaps to a place you would never have expected. Saying yes to something outlandish or out of your comfort zone may be the best thing you do.

A lot of people live in fear that prevents them from making bold decisions. You're too afraid to do something, so you do nothing. I know I've had times like this. The danger is that we begin to live in the land of "what if." *What if this happens? What if that happens? What if it all goes wrong?* Well, what if it all goes *right?* Had I stayed in fear of the plan Penny proposed to go to Kauai, I don't know where I would be today. Even though I was definitely worried about the lack of housing or a solid plan, I showed up and trusted that everything would fall into place. Of course, we still must use wisdom and not confuse foolishness with bravery. Looking back now, I'm glad the plan of staying with a stranger didn't work out. Probably God's protection!

Many of us come up with reasons and excuses to stall. But what if now is the time? The present moment is yours *now*. A lot of us squander dreams and desires because we're waiting for some magical moment to show up, when really, that moment is now. Sure, maybe you need to save up more money, pray about it longer, find an open weekend, or ask a business partner to help, but if you want something bad enough, you'll make it happen. You'll start moving toward that dream now. Don't let fear or a list of obstacles stop you from pursuing your dreams and desires.

I remember when I was sitting bored at home during the pandemic, and I thought about starting a podcast. I made a list of excuses as to why it wasn't the right time: *I don't know what to call it. I don't have a studio for it. No photographers can help me shoot a cover for it because of Covid. I don't have the right equipment. Heck, who am I to even start a podcast? Am I even qualified for this?*

Name an excuse, and I probably made it. But when I finally sat down and thought about this idea, I asked myself, "Do you want this or not?" And the answer was yes! I prayed about the right name, bought a cheap microphone on Amazon, took an old photo I had and put design over it in Photoshop for the cover, cranked out a ton of solo episodes, even asked friends to virtually come on my podcast, and I launched it! It wasn't perfect, lemme tell ya. The sound quality was rough, as was my webcam footage, but I did it! Because of that yes, my podcast has grown to have millions of listens, and I've had some of the most amazing people come on who have shared stories and wisdom with my wonderful listeners. I'm really not trying to brag, I promise, but rather encourage you to stop waiting for the right time to *just start*. It doesn't have to look perfect to begin—it usually won't—but keep going and letting yourself evolve.

Until you hit an actual legit *no*, keep going. And even if you hit a no, still keep going. I had many people not respond to my invitation to come on my podcast or tell me they didn't want to work with me. That may have hurt my ego a little bit, but it didn't stop me from believing in myself and the impact my podcast could make. So start the podcast, apply for that school, open the Etsy shop, book the trip, ask that person on a date, apply for the job, move to a new city—and just watch how life will unfold because of your courage and boldness. The only thing stopping you is *you*.

Maybe we all need a Penny in our lives—someone to push us and encourage us to live in fear less. But don't wait around for others to join or invite you to begin. You can begin now, all by yourself! This is your sign.

Saying Yes Makes Life More Fun

I have learned that by saying yes and trying new things, my life has become exceedingly richer. When I say rich, I don't mean financially, but more exciting and full. You never know what you'll discover and learn by trying something new. Before going on my Hawaii trip, I wasn't much of an adventurous person. At all. My sisters would tell you the same thing. Outside wasn't really my vibe, you could say. I was accustomed to city life and had never tried anything else. I was not being open-minded or giving new opportunities a chance. But when I began to say yes more, I started to try things I had never done before, like surfing, skateboarding, snowboarding, fishing, hiking, painting, and camping. To my surprise, I loved them all! Was I good at them all? Nope, but it didn't stop me from trying. Now I continue to do many of these activities, which has led me to meet incredible people in incredible places.

Be willing to look funny or dumb in the process of trying new things. No one should expect you to pick something up immediately, so don't put pressure on yourself to instantly be a pro or do it forever. The point is to say yes to trying new things, have fun, and gain new experiences.

One bold decision could have the power to create an entirely new passion and life for you. What if by taking a painting class you realized you are pretty good at painting, and now you sell your art online as a part-time job? Or by learning a new language, you now get to travel to a country that speaks that language and learn more about the culture. Or you take a spin class and realize it's your favorite way to work out, and eventually you teach spin classes. Or you say yes to something you feel God is calling you to, even though you are nervous, but it grows your faith and trust in him.

The possibilities are endless.

Give yourself space and an environment where it's safe to try, fail, learn, and innovate. I'd rather see you try and fail than not try at all. When I decided to try snowboarding in 2021, I was horrible. I fell—a lot. I once fell so bad that I bruised my tailbone, an injury that lasted a year. I kid you not. Sitting, working out, and using the bathroom were all painful. But I was determined to keep going despite my embarrassing wipeout. I watched a ton of YouTube videos on how to do it, asked people I knew for advice, and kept going. Now it's something I do regularly and absolutely love. Getting good at things takes time, and I still have so much to learn. Many people actually discouraged me from trying it and told me I should stick to skiing, since I'm a girl and it's too late to learn snowboarding. But honestly, that pushback only gave me motivation to keep trying more. If someone tells you that you can't, show them that you can. Let's talk about that next.

People in the Process

Here's the deal: people play a big factor in whether we do something or don't. Maybe there's something you've been dying to try or feel you might be good at, but others' opinions and lack of courage hold you back. When I started my YouTube channel in 2010, I was mortified when people would make fun of me for posting videos online. All I wanted to do was run and hide in a closet when someone mentioned it to me. But regardless of people's opinions, I loved it and kept going, and it eventually turned into my career. I don't know what that is for you—and your newest pursuit may simply become your favorite hobby, not necessarily a career—but don't quit. Don't let people's opinions prevent you from pursuing your dreams. People will always have something to say, but not everyone gets a say in what you do.

Your hobby, dream, talent, skill, or career might not make sense to them, and it doesn't have to. You'll find the right people along the way who will get it. I would hate for you to get to the end of your life and wish you had done more things that brought you joy, but didn't, because of people's opinions or expectations of you.

In a book by Bronnie Ware called *The Top Five Regrets of the Dying*, she shares what she learned from working with dying people for eight years. Not to get too dark on you, but she asked many of them what they wished they did in their life before passing, and she summarized the responses in the five following points:

"I wish I'd had the courage to live a life true to myself, not the life others expected of me."

"I wish I hadn't worked so hard."

"I wish I'd had the courage to express my feelings."

"I wish I had stayed in touch with my friends."

"I wish I had let myself be happier."[1]

Notice how they said they wished they had lived a life truer to themselves and let themselves be happier. So many of us are fearful of going against the grain or pursuing a passion either out of fear of others' opinions or fear of failure. Saying yes doesn't always have to be overly radical, but it's doing something for yourself that you've been putting off for a while.

This could mean finally pursuing a longtime passion of yours, moving somewhere you've always dreamed of, painting and redecorating your room, or quitting your job in hopes of starting a nonprofit—you name what that is for you! I can't imagine not doing my job now, even though others found it to be weird and different. You just never know where it will take you. In whatever you do, of course still use wisdom, seek counsel, and obey God, but if you genuinely love it, press on and see what happens. I am not trying to encourage a life of selfishness or a life only revolving around seeking temporal pleasures, but a life that takes chances and makes bold decisions that lead to achieving your wildest dreams. Imagine where you could be next year if you start now. Imagine who you could become and meet along the journey.

What if your yes to trying something new leads to forming a whole new community through your new endeavor? Maybe you meet an entirely new friend group by joining a group you've always wanted to. Or you meet people similar to you who motivate and inspire you in your passion. Or you meet your future spouse by moving to a new city you've dreamt of for a long time. I'm not sure what will happen, but what I do know is that anything could happen. That excites me! Take the risk or lose the chance.

Working through the Limitations

Now I know, you might be thinking about the limitations. *I don't have the time or money to say yes to everything, Jeanine.* And you would be right; none of us do! But in some seasons you may have more capacity to say yes to things than in others. You don't have to say yes to *everything*. It can be saying one yes per month to something new or something you're genuinely excited about. If you say yes, let it be a *heck yes!* Make a list of what that would be for you and start with that.

Typically for me, my list includes spontaneous trips with my friends, cool work events, and hosting gatherings at my house. But I still have to prioritize them and make space for them in my calendar, otherwise nothing happens at all. Don't think this is me telling you to throw every responsibility out the window to live in a van forever, but maybe for a weekend . . . Use your best wisdom and discernment as to when you can create margins in your time and save up money for those adventures. I recently stumbled across this TikTok video where a man interviewed elders and asked them what they regretted in life, and most of them said something like, "I wish I traveled when I was younger. I didn't because I always thought there would be a better opportunity down the road and there never was. I should have just gone, even if it meant staying in a cheaper, less nice place." The opportunity is now and today! Don't look back on life and wish you did more when you still had the chance.

Saying yes, however, doesn't only have to come in the form of travel or adventures, since I know these are more costly. There are so many things you can try within your own city, such as classes or a new hobby. It may require more effort than income, like going to a free workout class at your local park. But if you are like me and absolutely love to travel, don't have a limited mindset. Many apps and websites like Going, Hopper, or even Google Flights will show you the cheapest flights and the best times to fly. I've done this several times, actually. I type in a date that I'm free and see what places are the cheapest to fly to around that time. My friend group and I one time found $120 round trip tickets to Hawaii based on a deal from Southwest Airlines. We snatched it up! If you're able to, create some margin for adventures in your bank savings account so you have money that goes specifically toward new experiences. Keep in mind that with these deals, you'll have to book on the spot and be willing to go on a very specific date, but if you have flexibility and can do it with your work and lifestyle, then go for it!

I also buy flights with credit card points, so then I basically fly for free. Pretty cool, huh? I also use Expedia.com or credit card points to book hotels, so I save even more money. On a smaller scale, Groupon has deals for classes, restaurants, and tours all the time, pretty much no matter where you are in the U.S. Your girl is trying to save us both some coins! It may take a little more effort, but there are so many options.

HOW TO TRAVEL ON A BUDGET

Book flights with the following resources

1. Google Flights
2. Going.com
3. Expedia Rewards—according to Expedia, the best day of the week to buy your airline ticket is on Sunday
4. Credit card points—Chase Sapphire, Capital One, or Amex
5. Southwest Airlines deals

Save money with these tips

1. Travel out of season
2. Travel on weekdays instead of weekends
3. Save up points by flying with one airline consistently
4. Pack a carry-on to avoid luggage fees
5. Embrace hostels
6. Use public transportation
7. Ask locals for their hole-in-the-wall food recommendations rather than expensive restaurants you find online

If you simply cannot afford a flight or several days off work, that's okay! Never forsake the possibilities around you in neighboring states or countries, depending on where you live. Pack your bags, load up your car, get a good playlist going, and set off for a weekend getaway. I hope if you do, you'll share with me online so I can hear about your adventure.

Be wise and safe, but don't let fear hold you back any longer. Living a happier life includes trying new experiences and being grateful you get to. Many people might wish they could, but due to several reasons, they never do. Soak up the moment and create memories! Journal through your experience and write down what it taught you. Reflect on it and humbly share it with someone. Make every day an adventure—whether at home or abroad. There is so much life to be lived, and lived fully.

I hope this chapter has inspired you to go after the things you want, create the life you desire, and expect the unexpected. Don't live in fear any longer. Chase after the things you want and don't let one door closing stop you. I'm excited to see what your *yes* may lead to!

MAKE IT REAL IN YOUR LIFE

1. What is a new experience you've been wanting to try?
2. When was the last time you said yes to something that positively impacted you?
3. What excuses are you making that prevent you from pursuing a dream?
4. What is something you failed at but were thankful you tried?
5. Whose negative opinions stop you from saying yes more? What are they telling you?

---— 14 ——---

Satisfaction

How to Find the True Fulfilment You're Looking For

Growing up, my parents used to say to my six siblings and me, "No matter what you do, seek the Lord in everything. God is where you will always find true joy and life." Even though I didn't care for that advice at the time, eventually it came back to me and I began to see it was true. All my life, I was told Jesus was the answer, but it was almost like I didn't want to believe it because it seemed too easy or cheesy. I wondered if the answer could be found anywhere else. I wanted to taste and see what the world offered—and I did. I went to Los Angeles, pursued my dreams, made money, partied in Hollywood, met celebrities, traveled the world, made it on shows, got in a magazine, earned so-called fame—and yet, to my surprise, I still felt dissatisfied and empty. *Who would've thought?* Unfortunately, it took me testing it all out to find it wasn't what it was cracked up to be.

The fun that the world offered to me never really was that fun. Sure, it was cool in the moment, but being hungover the next day and forgetting what I did the night before always left this lingering feeling of guilt and regret. On the outside looking in, it appeared I was thriving, yet I had no real friends or sense of self, even though I was searching for them (just in all the wrong places). I was looking for fulfillment and purpose, but despite all my striving, I kept coming short and falling on my face with the overwhelming feeling of never being enough. Every. Single. Time. It was draining. I felt that way for many years. Anyone else?

Here's some good news: you don't have to get it right all the time. You can stop striving. You don't have to do this alone anymore. You don't have to be perfect. You don't have to wonder *Am I enough?* anymore. Why? Because Jesus is already *enough* for you. He is already perfect, so we don't have to be. *Phew.* We, as mere humans, can look to him to be the strength in our weaknesses. The apostle Paul shares God's response to him in 2 Corinthians 12:9 (emphasis added): "But he said to me, 'My grace is **sufficient** for you, for my power is made perfect in weakness.' Therefore, I will boast all the more gladly about my weaknesses, so that Christ's power may rest on me." Jesus is sufficient for us, even in our weaknesses. Amid all our failures, hurts, hang-ups, and regrets, Jesus is our strength and the solution in all our weaknesses.

Can I get an amen?

Our happiness and health are no longer solely dependent on us getting it right or manifesting a perfect life. Apart from God, we'll never fully get it anyway. Sure, we can get momentary moments of pleasure and happiness, but they always eventually run out, leaving us looking for the next high. We were never meant to be our own sustainer and source of joy and life. That has been God's role from day one. We'll always come out short if we try to be our own provider of happiness and wholeness. Deep down, our souls have heaven and eternity written on them. We long for safety and security from our Creator. We crave something bigger than us to guide us and keep us. Thankfully, we have the solution to our longing.

If you don't believe me and think you just have to do more and try more to feel fulfilled and accomplished, I just want to ask you to reflect on your past and ask yourself if it's working.

My hunch is, it's probably not—just like it wasn't for me. No matter what I did, how hard I tried, or the success I achieved, I still didn't feel fulfilled. No amount of striving in our own strength will result in us getting everything right. And I'm here to tell you:

That. Is. Okay.

You don't need to lay heavy, unrealistic burdens on yourself anymore. You can look to him to take them from you and help you manage them. The truth is, none of us will ever get everything perfectly right. I still don't get it right a lot of the time. I still struggle and have doubts, fears, and insecurities, but I know that I don't have to have it all together. I don't have to perform for God to earn his love, be *on* all the time, and constantly succeed to be accepted, and neither do you. I can rest knowing that God has my life and future in his hands, and he has yours too. I'm not extra special to God just because I'm writing a book; he has good plans too for you and your future. Quit the striving, and start abiding. All you have to do is abide in him and everything else will fall into place.

I hope as you go along in this process, you come to your desires and burdens from a place of knowing that whatever you need or desire that aligns with God's will, he will supply it according to his riches and glory (see Philippians 4:19). By abiding in God, you'll have all you need and more. *Abiding* means to remain, to dwell, stay connected to him, and make him your safe place in *all* you do. Jesus says, "I am the vine; you are the branches. Whoever abides in me and I in him, he it is that bears much fruit, for apart from me you can do *nothing*" (John 15:5 ESV, emphasis added). So before you enter into a relationship, or experience anxiety, face confusion, or even have high moments where you don't feel like you need God, abide in him even more. Run to him. Cry to him. Pray to him. Ask him first. Seek him in all your questions or fears. By doing so, you will find all that you need (Matthew 6:33).

I didn't write this book because I wanted to give you an exasperating list of new things to do but, instead, because I genuinely believe a lot of us sell ourselves short. We were made for more. We

181

limit ourselves so much more than God does. We can have a life of abundance, success, health, blessings, and goodness despite challenges and opposition. We often just don't know how to get there. My hope is that by sharing part of my story—both the hard parts and the good parts—I've passed on some motivation to pursue a happy and healthy life through Christ.

Before you go rushing off trying to fix all your problems and make things happen on your own, make him your foundation, motivation, and strength. Pause and ask yourself, do you want a life that points to God and says, "Look at God and what he did"? Or do you want it to say, "Look at me and what I did"? A life built on him, not yourself, will not waver.

No matter what happens in your life—whether you become rich or successful, buy a bigger house or nicer car, become well-known or marry the ideal person—never forget your first Love. You will do amazing things, but never forget to give thanks and glory to him.

Let him be the reason you smile, succeed, and set off to do big things. In my own journey, I would never have gotten where I am without Christ. I wouldn't have a story of victory because I'd still be stuck in my sin and unhealthy habits. Only by the saving grace of Jesus am I able to write this book and show you that the truths in his Word genuinely work for the good of those who love him (Romans 8:28). By applying Scripture to my life and practicing good habits, I have been transformed from addicted and ashamed to free and fulfilled. I may have fallen and failed many times, but I got back up, and I know you can too!

Don't waste another second living in shame, regret, and your past. Your life and time here on earth are too precious to squander. Imagine where you could be a year from now if you relentlessly seek God in all your wildest dreams and desires. He has so much in store for you! This is just the beginning.

Give yourself grace as you become more like Christ in this journey, because change doesn't happen overnight. Be proud of yourself for every small, positive change you make. I pray your life becomes increasingly blessed by seeking Jesus in all you do. I pray that your faith deepens, you find amazing people around you, you live a life of abundance, you succeed, you say yes more, and you become more confident in who God made you to be. May you thrive in whatever endeavor you touch, and may you become the freest, most fulfilled version of yourself. You have all the tools to become happy and healthy now. Go after it!

Stay happy and healthy.

—*Love, Jeanine*

MAKE IT REAL IN YOUR LIFE

1. How will you abide in Jesus today?
2. What are three areas you need the most growth in?
3. What is an area you see yourself constantly striving in but falling short?
4. In what ways do you think you're not enough? What does God say about that?
5. What would it look like for you to be happier and healthier?

Acknowledgments

Mommy and Daddy: thank you for raising me the way you did. For instilling God's love, truth, and faith in me. I could never have written this book without all the lessons you've taught me. Thank you for believing in me and supporting my wild dreams. You both are always there for me and are my biggest prayer warriors. I love you both so much.

My siblings: I love you all so much! Thank you for always being a part of my ideas, encouraging me to dream, praying for me when it was hard, and helping me be a better person. You all have played a massive role in my life, and I'm beyond grateful for you all.

Kaleb Ward: my now husband. We were just dating when I began writing this book, and you are now my husband. Thank you for sitting endlessly with me as I read these chapters to you, praying with me, encouraging me, and helping me along the way. I couldn't have done this without you!

Kacey Meairs: you are a massive reason why my life turned around. Thank you for speaking truth to me, helping me know God, challenging me, and showing me how to fall in love with Jesus. You've changed my life.

Madison Prewett Troutt: my best friend, my old roomie, my prayer warrior, and my biggest support. I cannot begin to thank you enough. Thank you for showing me how to have bold faith and be strong in your convictions. You've made me a better person and make me look more like Jesus. You supported me through this whole process, and it means the world to me. Thank you for taking the time to be my foreword writer as well. It's an honor to have my best friend open my book for me!

Riley Kehoe: my best friend and interceder. Your encouragement and prayer carried me through. Thank you for seeing the gifts in me and encouraging them. Your friendship and love of Jesus inspire me, motivate me, and make me love Jesus more.

Alyssa Farraye: beyond thankful for you. You've kept me so consistent in my journey. You were with me as I grew. You encouraged me, did life with me, and made me feel so safe. You are my best friend, and you've been an amazing prayerful friend.

Penny Paranka: my partner in crime. You've been there since day one and have seen me on this journey. Thank you for always seeing my potential and challenging me to get there. You've always believed in me and pushed me to be better. I appreciate your constant wisdom, positivity, and encouragement to me.

Jennie Allen: you are an incredible leader who challenged me in my faith so much and called me higher. Thank you for leading this generation and pouring into me. Thank you for believing in me and paving the way for me to know what a strong, godly woman looks like. You have truly pushed me back to Christ.

Jonathan Pokluda: I'm not sure how much you know you've impacted my life, but you have greatly. Thank you for consistently speaking truth, caring about my life, cheering me on, and being an incredible leader to this generation. Your life and boldness have helped me become who I am today.

My collaborator: thank you for all your help, support, time, and advice. I genuinely couldn't have done this process without you.

Bethany House: thank you guys for taking a chance on me and believing in me! I felt so supported all along the way. I couldn't have written this book without you.

Acknowledgments

My followers: so many of you have been with me throughout this whole journey, and I just want to say thank you. Thank you for believing in me, supporting me, caring about me, and reading this book. You are why I do what I do! I genuinely hope this book blesses you, and I'm eternally grateful for you all!

Notes

Introduction

1. Ellen Brown, "Writing is Third Career for Morrison," *The Cincinnati Enquirer*, September 27, 1981, https://www.newspapers.com/clip/21863475/tonimorrison/.

Chapter 2 Expectations: When You Feel You're Falling Behind

1. Brené Brown, *Rising Strong: The Reckoning. The Rumble. The Revolution* (New York: Random House, 2017), 139.

Chapter 3 Contentment: How to Keep Your Joy, Even When You're Alone

1. Jonathan Pokluda, interview by Jeanine Amapola, "Why Can't I Stop Sinning ft. Jonathon Pokluda," *Happy and Healthy*, April 25, 2023, video and podcast, 34:01, https://www.youtube.com/watch?v=EB6FSHzCnLg.

Chapter 5 Dating: How to Date in a Godly Way

1. Jonathan Pokluda, interview by Jeanine Amapola, "Why Can't I Stop Sinning ft. Jonathon Pokluda," *Happy and Healthy*, April 25, 2023, video and podcast, 34:01, https://www.youtube.com/watch?v=EB6FSHzCnLg.

2. Scott Edwards, "Love and the Brain," *On the Brain*, Spring 2015, https://hms.harvard.edu/news-events/publications-archive/brain/love-brain.

Chapter 6 Confidence: Overcoming Insecurities and Becoming Secure

1. Shameika Rhymes, "7 Ways to Make Better, More Confident Eye Contact," InHerSight, June 8, 2021, https://www.inhersight.com/blog/career-development/eye-contact.

2. Rhymes, "7 Ways to Make Better, More Confident Eye Contact."

Chapter 7 Habits: A Guide to Improve Your Day and Life

1. James Clear, *Atomic Habits: An Easy & Proven Way to Build Good Habits & Break Bad Ones* (New York: Penguin Random House, 2018), 15.

2. Clear, *Atomic Habits*, 39.

3. Phillippa Lally, Cornelia H. M. van Jaarsveld, Henry W. W. Potts, Jane Wardle, "How Are Habits Formed: Modelling Habit Formation in the Real World," *European Journal of Social Psychology*, July 16, 2009, https://doi.org/10.1002/ejsp.674.

Chapter 12 Wellness: How to Take Care of Yourself from the Inside Out

1. Caroline Leaf, "Dr. Carolyn [sic] Leaf Teaches Us How to 'Switch On Your Brain,'" interview by Kevin Scott, *100Huntley,* 100 Huntley Street, January 8, 2015, YouTube video, 3:16, https://youtu.be/OPmlw0qgVy4.

2. Julie Tseng and Jordan Poppenk, "Brain Meta-State Transitions Demarcate Thoughts Across Task Contexts Exposing the Mental Noise of Trait Neuroticism," *Nature Communications* 11, 3480 (2020), https://doi.org/10.1038/s41467-020-17255-9.

3. Mayo Clinic Staff, "Water: How Much Should You Drink Every Day?" Mayo Clinic, October 12, 2022, https://www.mayoclinic.org/healthy-lifestyle/nutrition-and-healthy-eating/in-depth/water/art-20044256.

4. "Giving Thanks Can Make You Happier," Harvard Health Publishing, August 14, 2021, https://www.health.harvard.edu/healthbeat/giving-thanks-can-make-you-happier.

Chapter 13 Adventure: How to Embrace New Experiences

1. Bronnie Ware, *The Top Five Regrets of the Dying: A Life Transformed by the Dearly Departing* (Carlsbad, CA: Hay House, 2012).

Jeanine Amapola is an author, podcast host, speaker, and Christian influencer based out of Dallas, Texas. She graduated from the University of Texas at Austin with a communications major and business minor and now does social media and podcasting full time. She has been in the social media industry for over a decade and has garnered over 2.7 million followers across all her platforms. She loves to post topics regarding faith, identity, dating, confidence, health, lifestyle, and more.

Jeanine is passionate about helping women all across the world know Jesus more and become happy and healthy in all aspects of life—mentally, physically, spiritually, and emotionally—through God's Word and daily habits.

Learn more at YouTube.com/@JeanineAmapola, Instagram.com /JeanineAmapola, and YouTube.com/c/HappyandHealthyPodcast